Conquering Chronic Disorganization

JUDITH KOLBERG

Squall Press, Inc.

P.O. Box 691
Decatur, GA 30031

Copyright © 1998
First Printing 1999
Manufactured in the United States of America
Text and Cover Design by Stephanie Troncalli
Product Photography by Clint Alexander
Editing by Adrian Fillion
FIRST EDITION
10 9 8 7

Library of Congress Catalog Card Number
98-91023

Squall Press, Inc.

P.O. Box 691
Decatur, GA 30031

Praise for *Conquering Chronic Disorganization*

I highly recommend this book to anyone who has failed to find organizing solutions in conventional organizing books. – Jerri Udelson, Vice President, International Coach Federation, NE

Conquering paints a vivid and poignant picture of chronic disorganization, filled with humor and imagination. I find its inventiveness inspiring. And it's just plain fun to read! – Pipi Campbell Peterson, Author, *Ready, Set, Organize!*

I've read every book on organizing there is, and this is the only book that has ever made any real difference for me. – Nathan Argon, Director, Quality Communications

Chronic disorganization was wrecking my life. Kolberg turned me around. – Jessica Walton, President, Cyberlife, Inc.

I predict this book will become the Bible of organizing books for anyone who is disorganized or anyone who wants to help someone who is disorganized. – Ann Weinfeld Saunders, LCSW-C, Professional Organizer, Baltimore, MD

A must for everyone who is challenged by disorganization. – Sandra Felton, Author, *Messy No More*

Conquering is a pioneering work. It offers practical help and takes into account differences between people. I will be recommending it to my chronically disorganized clients as well as using some of its practical suggestions myself. – Ann McAllister, PhD, Psychologist and Professional Coach

Dedication

This book is dedicated to Eleanor Kolberg, my mother,
for all her loving support and encouragement.

"There was a man
and some did think him mad.
The more he cast away,
the more he had."
Pilgrim's Progress

Acknowledgments

Special thanks to the members of the National Study Group on Chronic Disorganization for providing me with a context in which to fly my ideas, especially Sandra Felton, Denslow Brown, Jerri Udelson, and Betsy Wilkowsky. Many thanks to Penny Walker, Shea McNutt, and Adrian Fillion for their word-processing and editing help. I am also grateful to Don Aslett and Dorothy Lehmkuhl for their kind words of encouragement. Also, I appreciate Hariette Gershon and Joyce Tierney for their assistance in the promotion of this book. And finally, to Linda McGuire for never flinching in her support of me.

TABLE of CONTENTS

WHAT IS CHRONIC DISORGANIZATION?

Call 911!!   Call 911!!

Marie is a very successful real estate broker. Recently awarded a Million Dollar Agent Award for the fifth year in a row, she stands out as a star even in Atlanta, where brokers are plentiful and the real estate market is as hot as a summer without air conditioning. For fifteen years Marie has led the pack. When Marie called me to help her get organized, I immediately recognized her name from the yard signs I had seen stuck in the sod of dozens of regal homes. Though I knew her name, I did not know the circumstances that prompted Marie's call.

It seems that Marie's regular maid had to leave town suddenly to attend to a family crisis in Macon. Unsure when the maid would return, Marie was frantic. The holidays were approaching, unexpected guests were more than likely to drop by, and the house desperately needed cleaning. A colleague of Marie's recommended a maid service, and a substitute maid was retained.

Real estate brokers, even well-to-do brokers like Marie, work at a very hectic pace to move that next million dollar home off a recalcitrant market. It is typical for Marie to be "out in the field", on her car phone, meeting with prospective buyers, or at the corporate office filling in the blanks of yet another signed contract, rather than at her home office. It is not unusual for busy Atlantans to arrange for maids and other service providers to let themselves in.

New to the job and eager to impress, the maid followed Marie's instructions to the letter. She drove up the long drive of the palatial home to the rear of the house and parked. She climbed the three wooden stairs of the rear deck and found the terra-cotta urn as directed. Tilting it slightly, underneath she found the key to the back door. (Atlanta simply refuses to believe it is one of the murder capitals of the world. In true Southern hospitality style, she still keeps her extra key hidden on the back porch.)

The maid opened the back door to Marie's home and found herself in a hallway. Two doors stood opposite each other on either side of the hall. One door opened to the guest bedroom where the cleaning was to begin. The other door led to Marie's home office, which the maid had been instructed to avoid. In a moment of confusion, the maid forgot which door was which. She entered the home office door.

She stopped dead in her tracks. Her jaw dropped, her heartbeat quickened, and her cleaning bucket slipped from her hand. With her eyes widened, she could not help but take in the entire view in front of her. The room was totally ransacked. The desk was strewn with papers so thick the surface of the desk was not visible. Stacking trays were toppled. Piles of documents had slithered from the desk to the floor like lava. The filing cabinet drawers were pulled open and file folders and loose papers gushed over the sides of the drawers. The credenza was slathered with opened binders, and documents teetered on the edge. The couch was covered with papers, and the floor revealed but one small pathway from the door to the desk.

So plundered was the appearance of the office that the maid concluded the house had been vandalized. In a panic, believing the perpetrator might still be inside, she fled to the leasing office of Marie's subdivision. With arms flailing in the air, she screamed "Call 911! Call 911!" The office manager was able to get sketchy details from the hysterical maid and promptly called the police. She also contacted Marie in her car and broke the news of the crime to her.

Marie raced home. She bounded out of her BMW and joined the maid and office manager outside the door to her home office. Police were inside taking photographs and sprinkling fine dust on the door-knob in an effort to find fingerprints. Marie gazed inside and concluded that nothing really was out of place at all. However, seeing the blue police lights spinning, the diligence of the detectives, and the distraught maid before her, Marie thought it better to keep this realization to herself. Slightly dazed, she mechanically accepted a clipboard handed her by a policeman and replied with a wooden "Yes" to the request that she fill out a missing property report.

The maid calmed, and the police dismissed, Marie walked slowly into her home office, slid some papers from her desk chair, and plopped down exasperated. Rummaging through the top drawer of her desk, she managed to find a two-year-old business card (mine) and called me to relay this story.

"It's so embarrassing!" Marie told me over the phone. "But it has always been this way for me. I remember in college I had three different dormitory roommates in one year! They would all move out on me. When my little study desk was too covered with papers I would simply start stacks on the floor. When that was full, I would continue stacking on the bed, and even the ironing board! Since college, I must have gone through a dozen file clerks and secretaries. I've tried everything – filing cabinets, in-boxes, color-coding, and I've probably bought every kind of organizing gizmo ever made. I might get organized for a little while, then boom, things are right back where they were again…and now this," she sighed with resignation.

SAVING GRACE

Grace's husband Art telephoned me one June day. An older Southern gentleman, Art told me he and Grace had been married thirty-seven years, had raised three wonderful children, and simply adored their eleven grandchildren. Now that Grace has joined him in retirement, he thought they would "get their ducks all in a row," a terrific Southern expression for getting organized. Art continued to provide me with details about their life together and their future plans, and I began to wonder why he had phoned me. Everything he described sounded so perfect.

Just then Art's voice dropped to a whisper and for a moment I thought something had gone wrong with the phone. "I share my home with 364 margarine tubs," Art whispered.

"Excuse me? Did you say 'margarine tubs'?" I asked not quite believing my ears. "Yes, margarine tubs, and they occupy all of our kitchen cupboard space," Art went on. "Not only that, but Grace also saves every plastic bag and paper bag she gets at the market. It started when the kids were small, and I admired her thrift, but now all this stuff clutters up the house. She just can't seem to throw things away. I call her Saving Grace," Art continued in a low, soft voice as if speaking from inside a closet.

"Once I took her to a recycling plant, thinking that if she knew margarine tubs could become something of value she might give them up. She recycled for a little while but gave it up. I even went with her to a Tupperware party! I was the only guy there! It was so embarrassing. But I thought if she bought the good stuff, she might let the tubs go. She bought the good stuff, alright, but kept right on saving the bags and tubs. Now that Grace is retired and will have more time on her hands, I'm worried. We're running out of space." Art whispered, "Can you help Grace?"

"Does Grace know you are calling me?" I asked, half expecting Grace to catch Art and me on the phone. Surely, given the way we were conversing, she would accuse him of having an affair.

"No. Grace is at the store getting groceries…and more bags!" Art exclaimed.

WHAT IS CHRONIC DISORGANIZATION?

Marie and Grace are not just disorganized, they are chronically disorganized. Chronically disorganized people have a persistent problem with disorganization. It is a constant battle and seems to endure no matter what. In fact, the dictionary's synonyms for "chronic" are "persistent," "constant," and "enduring." Chronic disorganization is disorganization that has a long history, undermines one's quality of life on a daily basis, and recurs.

Chronic Disorganization Is Disorganization That Has A Long History

Nearly all her adult life, Grace has had trouble parting with residential clutter. When Grace and I met, she told me:

"My sister visited, and she and my niece and I organized the house. We threw out things I haven't used for years. It felt good. We organized all the dishes and glasses and pots and pans. I had Art build a shelf and on it we stacked plastic containers, like margarine tubs. I folded up my paper garbage bags and neatly placed them behind the refrigerator. I threw away a bunch of plastic bags and kept a small supply in the broom closet. But within a few months, it was exactly like we never did anything! Bags stuck out every which way from behind the refrigerator. The shelves were all jumbled up again. The plastic bags took over all the space in the broom closet, and I had accumulated so many margarine tubs Art had to build two more shelves! I'm sure my sister and niece think I am unappreciative of their help. Art thinks I'm lazy or crazy. Maybe he's right!"

Chronic Disorganization Undermines Quality of Life on a Daily Basis

Clearly Grace's quality of life is undermined by the chronic level of her disorganization. Clutter causes discomfort to one's self, family members, friends, and co-workers.

Marie calls her own office "a foreign country." "I might just as well be a tourist," Marie confesses. "I can never find what I need when I need it. Every day I waste time looking for lost documents. This makes me late for appointments and unprepared for meetings."

Each and every day, chronic disorganization belittles one's quality of life. It creates daily stress and anxiety. Left unaddressed, chronic disorganization can threaten job security, injure relationships, and lower self-esteem.

Chronic Disorganization Recurs

But the most pernicious feature of chronic disorganization is its "chronicness." Marie and Grace have tried to get organized. In her organizing arsenal, Marie includes numerous filing cabinets, assorted in-boxes, and an array of dayplanners. She has tried alphabetizing and categorizing. She has employed clerks, secretaries, and administrative assistants. Still, no matter how valiant the try, that just-hit-by-a-tornado look returns to Marie's office after a few months. Grace gets overwhelmed before she even starts.

Grace has seen a therapist, used her family to help, and even attended a de-cluttering class. She manages to discard a few disposables, but they always seem to replenish themselves with a vengeance.

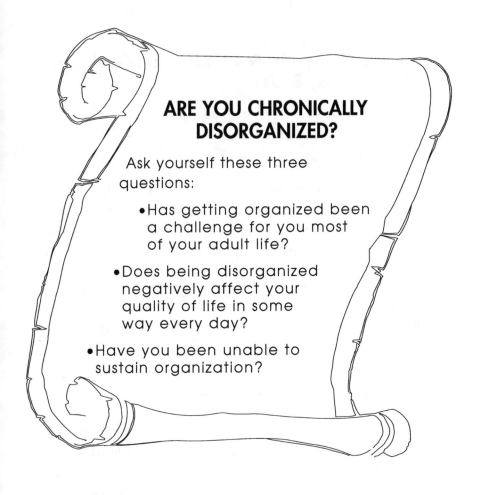

ARE YOU CHRONICALLY DISORGANIZED?

Ask yourself these three questions:

- Has getting organized been a challenge for you most of your adult life?

- Does being disorganized negatively affect your quality of life in some way every day?

- Have you been unable to sustain organization?

If you answered Yes to each of these questions, you are chronically disorganized. If you did not answer yes to all of them, you will still benefit from the organizing approaches and methods described in this book. After all, if they work for chronically disorganized people, imagine what they can do for you!

WHY ARE SOME PEOPLE CHRONICALLY DISORGANIZED?

I don't think Grace is crazy. And I don't think she or Marie is lazy. But it is interesting how most people, even people who hate getting organized, have been able to accomplish some level of organization in their lives and sustain it, while the level of organization for others deteriorates so badly it actually affects their quality of life. And yet, on any other score, the first group of people and the second group of people are alike. So why is getting and staying organized such a challenge for some people and not for others?

Most people organize conventionally. They are able to get organized and stay organized because they can respond to and benefit from conventional organizing methods. Conventional methods such as filing systems, storage systems, and time management systems have a certain logic to them. If you think, learn, and organize within the logic of those systems, getting and staying organized is possible.

But chronically disorganized people are not conventional. They think, learn, and organize in ways that are unconventional. Marie, for example, will not suddenly wake up one day, whack herself on the head, and say, "Now I get it. I finally realize how to file! I give a piece of paper a name or title or topic, I write that topic on a manila folder and I put the paper inside the manila folder. I find all the other papers with that same topic and put them inside also. Then I put all the manila folders inside a filing cabinet. Then I establish categories of topics, and file all the file folders by category inside the filing cabinet. If I pull a file folder out, I simply return it to its proper category when I am done."

Intellectually, Marie knows the filing drill. But the way she organizes, the way she actually thinks about her papers, defies conventional organizing! Marie has only the vaguest notion of what topic to assign any given piece of paper at any given time. She might assign it one topic one day and another topic the next day. So she cannot file or retrieve, at least not conventionally, because her frame of reference for her papers is not logic-based. You will discover, as I have, that there is indeed a method to Marie's madness. It turns out that Marie organizes her papers emotionally, not logically.

THE MYTH OF "ONCE AND FOR ALL"

Conventional organizing systems and methods are designed to be "once and for all" tools. But because we all do not organize the same way, the "for all" part of current methods leaves chronically disorganized people in a lurch. Marie is not a logical thinker, at least not when it comes to getting her papers organized. But the only organizing methods and tools currently available to her are those based on logic, and they fail her. **Chronic disorganization is the result of the bad fit between people who organize unconventionally and the very conventional organizing methods which exist for them to use.**

You might ask, why can't Marie organize conventionally? Why does logic not suit her? In all honesty, I do not know. Organizing, like all learned behaviors, is a very complex phenomenon. It involves the ways neurological information is processed; complicated sociological factors such as exposure to and integration of organizing skills; and psychological factors I could not even pretend to describe.

The breakthrough here is the recognition that we all do not organize the same way. Those of us who organize unconventionally, for whatever reason (and we may never really know the exact reason), need unconventional organizing methods, systems, and tools.

Chronic Disorganization Can Be Conquered

The radical organizing methods in this book have proven to be effective for getting chronically disorganized people organized. They provide a better fit for the unconventional ways in which chronically disorganized people think, learn, and organize. These radical methods also have another quality key to conquering chronic disorganization. We've explored the fallacy of the "for all" part of "once and for all". Well, the "once" part is also flawed.

If you are chronically disorganized, not only has disorganization characterized your past, but in all likelihood, it will mark your future. The reality is that the tendency to be disorganized is ever-present for chronically disorganized people. It is always imminent. Disorganization can return in a short period of time. You cannot get organized once and expect it to last. Perhaps this sounds contradictory to you. On the one hand, this is a book about conquering chronic disorganization. On the other hand, chronic disorganization is always imminent. Isn't the whole point about conquering chronic disorganization to put an end to it? Yes. But this cannot be achieved with conventional organizing approaches because they do not address the "chronicness" part of chronic disorganization. The radical methods contained in this book have "anti-chronic" devices built into them. These anti-chronic devices are designed to be weapons to conquer chronic disorganization.

Chronic disorganization can be conquered. It cannot be cured because it is not a disease. I want to make a special point about this because we live in an era that turns many human differences into medical problems. There is no known breakdown in the human body or mind that results in an organically based disease, deficiency, or disorder known as chronic disorganization. Chronic disorganization is not a medical condition. Sure, disorganization can accompany obsessive-compulsive disorder, clinical depression, and other mental illnesses. And if those illnesses are long-term, the attendant disorganization can be chronic. But we have in mind here chronic disorganization as a quality of life issue, not a medical condition.

EMOTIONAL ORGANIZING

ONCE MORE WITH FEELING

"Darn reports! This is nothing but public relations garbage put out by a lot of people who don't have enough to do. And look at this letter! I can't believe I haven't written back yet! And this stuff over here...my clients are always asking me for this, but do you think I can ever find it when I need it? No. Because I'm too disorganized." Marie finally finishes her tirade, and standing square in the middle of her office, knee-high in papers, asks, "So, are you going to teach me how to file now?"

"Certainly not," I respond.

"Well, what are we going to do?"

"We are going to continue to mutter."

"Mutter?" Marie exclaims, "What do you mean mutter?"

"Mutter. Like you are doing now. Just walk through your office and pick up papers and mutter the first thing that comes into your mind. This report, for example. You said it's 'nothing but public relations garbage.' And this letter, what did you say? Oh yes, 'I can't believe I haven't written back yet'."

"You're kidding," Marie says. "You really want me to keep ranting and raving?"

"Yes."

Marie stares at me for a moment but commences walking through her office with me trailing behind her with a stack of file folders in my arms. I write "Public Relations Garbage" on the tab of one file folder, and "I Can't Believe I Haven't Written Back Yet" on the tab of another, and place the appropriate papers inside. "I need to copy this," Marie says, waving a document in the air as I stand a pace behind, like Ms. Goosh in *Auntie Mame*. I rapidly write "I Need to Copy This" on a file folder and pluck the waved document from Marie's hand.

"In my dreams!" Marie exclaims as another paper flaps from her hand in my general direction. "In My Dreams" is a popular mutter folder. We have to use an expandable file to contain all the stuff of Marie's dreams. There is the promotional literature about the new computer Marie wants but cannot afford, and the decorating ideas that will have to wait, and all sorts of other items worthy of dreaming but not worth cluttering up the office.

"Why Can't I Find This When I Need It?" is an especially important mutter folder. Inside it we put those many single sheets of data and statistics and research information Marie always needs at some critical moment but can never find.

"I Wish I Had Thought Of That" is another handy mutter. It includes ideas other people have come up with that Marie thinks are smart, inventive, or profitable. She hopes to implement these ideas someday. "Have Got To Call These People" replaces a savage-looking spike driven through a wad of pink message pads. "This contraption sends out a distinct 'These calls are dead' message," Marie comments.

By far the most meaningful mutter is the file she calls "This Stuff Might Come Back To Haunt Me." Once it is created, Marie can hardly imagine how she ever lived without it.

Marie and I are able to mutter our way through the entire office. It takes six hours over two days. When we are finished, Marie's desk is reclaimed. Loose papers have disappeared from her credenza. The stacks on the floor are gone. The in-boxes have been retired. We plop down on her now-clear sofa. Marie stares out at the neat officescape before her and remarks, "I just can't believe it! Once before when I had my office organized this deeply, I went into a panic. It took me even longer to find what I was looking for because all my visual cues were gone. I relied on my papers being at certain angles or in certain spots. I even looked for distinguishing marks like coffee stains! So when they all disappeared from my view into file folders and then into filing cabinets, I panicked. But this feels so much different. My papers are gone but I know where they are. Each one 'lives' in a mutter folder I have created."

I am not as confident as Marie about her capacity to recall in what mutter folder individual documents are stored. So we perform a little test.

"Where is the list of termite inspectors?"

"Oh, that's easy. It's in 'Things Clients Bug Me For'."

"And what about the magazine clipping about genuine English lace tablecloths?" She thinks a moment and says, "In the 'Dreams' file!"

Marie is clearly an unconventional organizer. Her great capacity to function on a personal, emotional level makes her very much a "people-person" and has served her well as a realtor. But this same strength is a weakness when it comes to organization. Marie is now a successful paper manager because the Muttering Game optimizes her emotional orientation to the documentation which surrounds her.

You can play The Muttering Game too. The rules are easy. To get you started, below is a list of Suggested Mutterings…but don't be confined by them. They are just to get you started. Use your true feelings and reactions. Really let yourself go!

HOW TO PLAY THE MUTTERING GAME

Find yourself a Mutter Mate.

Supply your Mutter Mate with file folders with straight-cut tabs. They run the full length of the file folders (don't use 1/3 or 1/5 cut).

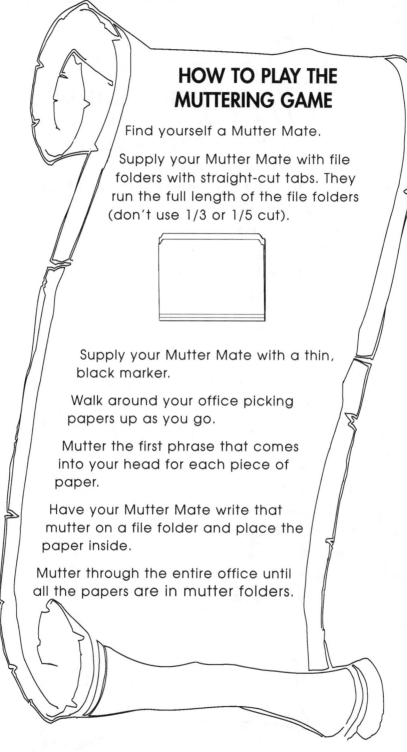

Supply your Mutter Mate with a thin, black marker.

Walk around your office picking papers up as you go.

Mutter the first phrase that comes into your head for each piece of paper.

Have your Mutter Mate write that mutter on a file folder and place the paper inside.

Mutter through the entire office until all the papers are in mutter folders.

SUGGESTED MUTTERINGS

This May Come Back To Haunt Me
Things My Clients Bug Me For
In My Dreams
Stuff I Can Never Find When I Need It
Good Ideas
Wish I Had Thought Of That
When I Win The Lottery
Not In This Lifetime
Treasures
Things I Feel Guilty About
If I Were A Rich Man/Woman
Sexy Stuff
I Have Got To Call These People
Proves My Point
Did I Get Paid For These Yet?
Bad Ideas
The Tax Man
Funny Stuff
This Makes Me Feel Good
Cover My Assets
Those Were The Days
Hostile Correspondence
Friendly Correspondence

Fear of Filing

Marie, like many chronically disorganized people, has a fear of filing. This fear is not a phobia, which is an irrational fear. It is, in fact, a rational fear. If you are an out-of-sight-out-of-mind person, you really *will* lose track of documents not in front of you. That is why so many chronically disorganized people stack and pile papers and do anything they can to be sure their documents do not disappear into the black hole of a filing cabinet drawer.

I have watched Marie attempt to retrieve a file from her filing cabinet. It is not a pretty sight. Her eyes glaze over. She is overcome with something akin to "refrigerator blindness," a malady common among teenage boys. Teenage boys open the refrigerator, lean in for a closer look, scan the contents, move nothing inside, and, amid the vast array of food, conclude there is nothing to eat and close the refrigerator door. They do not see the food. In this same way Marie does not "see" her filing system when it is contained in a filing cabinet.

We decide to organize the mutter folders in Panic Order, a very unconventional but effective emotional technique. Panic Order is the process of arranging file folders vertically on the desk according to the severity of what can go wrong. This is a highly personal and eccentric process. Marie chooses to put I Have Got To Call These People in the very first slot of the desktop file folder holder. It is followed by the file I Can't Believe I Haven't Written Back Yet. In Marie's mind, if she fails to make these calls or write these people, much can go wrong so she puts these files up front.

Arrange your desktop mutter files in Panic Order.

Marie's Panic Order files are all action-oriented. They represent, in emotional terms, things to do. Files that are not action-oriented are placed inside filing crates. Filing crates are those milk-carton-type plastic cubes readily available in office supply stores and discount stores. Unlike horizontal in-boxes, the filing crates hang files vertically. **The visibility of vertical is far superior to the hiddenness of horizontal.**

Crate on casters

I do want to point out that there are some kinds of files best arranged alphabetically or chronologically. These include client files and income tax file.

Find a Mutter Mate

How will Marie maintain her emotional filing system? What will it take for her to keep it up, knowing that disorganization is always barking at the door? Marie has a monthly Mutter Mate named Nancy. She is a young woman recently licensed in the field of real estate but not particularly interested in having her own company. She assists Marie with a variety of real estate tasks. The three of us met one afternoon, and Marie and I taught Nancy the Muttering Game. Once a month, Nancy and Marie play the Muttering Game and discard unneeded papers, create new emotional files as needed, and file loose papers.

Marie has successfully reorganized the paper management aspect of her life by moving away from logic-based filing systems and towards a system based more on emotions. Marie is pretty open with her emotions. Expressing herself comes naturally. Maybe that is why the Muttering Game works so well for her.

WHERE SHOULD I FILE MY NOBEL PRIZE?

Richard is not nearly as expressive as Marie. A research scientist at the Centers for Disease Control in Atlanta, Richard received a nomination for the Nobel Peace Prize for Medicine. I met him at a dinner given in his honor and it was clear from his remarks from the podium that Richard is a humble man, embarrassed by all the attention and not comfortable at all with making speeches. Later we somehow found ourselves standing next to each other, juggling little plates of hors d'oeuvres in one hand and drinks in the other. Richard is most interested in my expertise and invites me to his office.

The stacks of papers on Richard's desk completely obscure his view. He no longer even knows when someone has entered his office because he cannot see the door when seated at his desk. The piles of papers on the floor are limited only by gravity. When a stack begins to tilt from excessive height, the pile is simply cut in half like a deck of cards.

I am interested in discovering how Richard organizes his papers. I randomly pick up a document and notice it is from the IRS alerting Richard of an impending tax audit. I ask Richard where he might file this piece of paper. He studies it momentarily and responds, "I would file it under C." A for audit, I for IRS, and T for taxes come to my mind, but "C"? Well, I'm stumped. Richard explains that a very important client gave him a cat as a gift – a very expensive, pedigree cat. Apparently the cat became ill and Richard took it to a highly specialized veterinarian for treatment. Several doctor visits, injections, and an operation later, Richard received his bill from the veterinarian for a small fortune. Fond of the cat, Richard nonetheless resented the cost and deducted the expenses for caring for the cat as a client gift on his income taxes. He surmised the client gift entry on his taxes must have sent up a red flag to the IRS, and now he was being audited. "C stands for Cat," Richard says, unraveling the mystery.

Richard thinks about his papers in a very circuitous manner. One thought leads to another and then to another until pinning down a topic, subject, or title for anything is futile. Filing and retrieval are often difficult for chronically disorganized people whose thinking is circuitous, tangential, divergent, or in any other way unconventional. But emotional organizing can come to the rescue.

We create three generic *emotionally* oriented subject areas and dedicate one file drawer to each. "Keeping Me Out Of Jail" is the first. In it we file Richard's alimony payments, traffic tickets, and IRS audit notice. Everything in that drawer is related to the idea that if left unattended, Richard might be thrown in jail. The second drawer is labeled "Keeping People Off My Back," which contains items of less dire consequence, such as bills, reports, and other documents.

The third drawer is called "Me." The "Me" drawer stores the Nobel Prize nomination letter and other documents directly about Richard: media coverage, continuing education credits, and his numerous awards.

Richard can find most anything in ten minutes. Still his filing system is not one I would recommend even chronically disorganized people generally use. The subject areas are far too broad for most organizing situations. But I relay Richard's story because he is another example of how emotional organizing helps an unconventional organizer.

SAVING SAVING GRACE

In my entire ten years as a professional organizer, I have had a handful of clients who are hoarders with a diagnosed psychological problem called Obsessive Compulsive Disorder (OCD). But the vast majority of "packrats" like Grace simply have too much stuff for too long in too small a space for too many reasons. Grace is very articulate about her reasons for saving – her youth during the Great Depression, a history of deprivation, and a gratification for finding multiple purposes for things. Aware that her tendency to save is out of the norm, Grace briefly sought counseling. Counseling gave Grace even more insights about why she saves. Insensitive parents who threw away a precious toy prematurely; and the necessity of sharing everything with her many siblings were identified as two more reasons why Grace saves.

Among the many things Grace collects and saves are her insights and reasons for collecting and saving. In fact, along with the buttons and screws and macaroni that have found their way into Grace's margarine tubs, I half expect to see reasons and insights packed away, to be used when needed. I believe Grace's reasons for saving. I have no reason to doubt them. I also trust her insights, but the point is, Grace's insights do not help her to go beyond her current problem.

> In her book *I've Got To Get Rid of This Stuff*, Sandra Felton says: The problem of clutter, including hoarding, does not seem to yield well to this insight approach. You do not have to understand why you hoard in order to leave the morass you are in for an orderly, satisfying, supportive life-style free of clutter and the drive to collect. For some people, seeking this kind of understanding is a way of continuing to stall the hard job of changing. Although it may be helpful in many ways, traditional psychotherapy is not the best approach for overcoming the problem of hoarding.

I remind Grace I am no psychologist and can not begin to change her even if I wanted to. "All I want to do is change the way that you save. I have an idea. I know it's going to sound wacky at first but let's give it a try," I suggest.

"Okay, Sugar," Grace responds agreeably. (In the South, when someone calls you Sugar, it sounds like an endearment but it really means so much more. It means someone is putting all their trust in you. It is a very heavy responsibility to be called Sugar.)

Grace and I play an emotional organizing game I call Friends, Acquaintances, and Strangers. From among the 364 margarine tubs, Grace selects her one hundred Friends. I give her no criteria for choosing her Friends because it does not matter. What matters is that the personalized use of the term Friends allows Grace to distinguish some tubs from others and opens a small window of opportunity for narrowing down her collection.

We reshelve Grace's one hundred Friends and begin to work on the Strangers. I do suggest a criterion for Strangers. Grace is a friendly woman and it is said of her that she "knows no strangers." This is a Southern expression for making everyone you meet your friend. For this reason, I think it important for Grace to have some guidelines for what a Stranger is. "You would not want a Stranger in your house for long. That being the case, it's best to ask them to leave," I offer. Eighty-nine tubs make the cut as Strangers. If 100 Friends remain and only eighty-nine Strangers are discarded, then 175 Acquaintances still need to be contended with.

I wonder what emotional activity will prompt Grace to part with her Acquaintances. Recycling the tubs into Army boots holds no appeal for Grace. Perhaps something charitable will have a better effect.

Grace and I decide to go to church. I am Jewish and prefer to observe my own faith, but I have often been in churches, especially in the South. So much happens there! I have attended ecumenical peace services, business networking events, community prayer services for AIDS patients, and political rallies, all in churches.

This day, Grace and I are in church to meet the coordinator of a welfare mothers' organization. This organization provides proper interview attire to welfare mothers reentering the workforce. They also supply basic home furnishings. Welfare mothers are too poor to purchase Tupperware and too thrifty to throw away leftovers. Grace's tubs would be perfect. I get lucky. Grace hands over all 175 tubs, and her husband Art sends me a dozen roses!

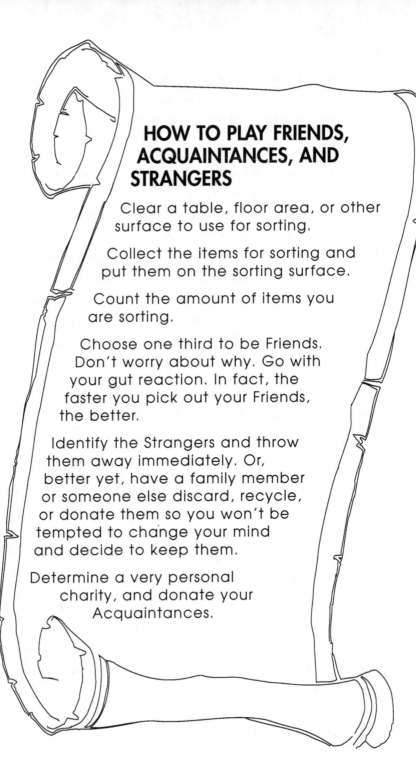

HOW TO PLAY FRIENDS, ACQUAINTANCES, AND STRANGERS

Clear a table, floor area, or other surface to use for sorting.

Collect the items for sorting and put them on the sorting surface.

Count the amount of items you are sorting.

Choose one third to be Friends. Don't worry about why. Go with your gut reaction. In fact, the faster you pick out your Friends, the better.

Identify the Strangers and throw them away immediately. Or, better yet, have a family member or someone else discard, recycle, or donate them so you won't be tempted to change your mind and decide to keep them.

Determine a very personal charity, and donate your Acquaintances.

The IN/OUT Ratio

I am concerned about Grace's collection rebuilding. Remember, she is chronically disorganized. Her tendency to save is ever-present. Three months from now, would Grace load up again on margarine tubs? In order to control Grace's stock of tubs at their new reduced level, she and I go into negotiations. Our negotiations seek a ratio of how many tubs to discard for every new tub added.

Grace is a tough negotiator. I propose ten tubs out for every one tub in. She counters with two tubs out for every one tub in. We finally agree that five tubs will be thrown away for every new one that is added. This In/Out ratio, plus the Friends, Acquaintances, and Strangers Game does the trick. Grace's tub collection is permanently controlled. Here are some In/Out ratios:

1:1 One old item out for every new item in will control your collection at its current level

1:2 Two old items out for every new item in will slowly diminish your old collection as you upgrade it with new items

1:3 Three old items out for every one item in will begin to replace your old collection with new items **and decrease** your overall collection

1:5 Five old items out for every new item in will decrease your overall collection **permanently** and leave you with only the very best of your existing collection.

Playing up Grace's emotional attachment to her margarine tubs with the game Friends, Acquaintances, and Strangers is a good example of how a "low need" accumulating behavior can be changed. By low need I mean margarine tubs and other impersonal items, what most of us would call disposables. Most people, even chronically disorganized people, have a low need to own a great number of disposables. But other items are quite personal. Clothes, mementos, and books are good examples of "high need" items. Hardly anyone wants to part with books because we feel more personal about them. The more personal an item is, the higher the need to keep it, or the lower the desire to part with it. So, how can you use emotional organizing when you are surrounded by high need things?

DOES THIS NEED ME?

Brian's book collection is massive and his apartment is small. Though he lives alone, he shares his apartment with a rather large dog. He loves the dog. He loves the books. Recently the dog backed into a bookcase, which came crashing down. Squealing like a pig, the dog narrowly escaped injury. Brian spent the better part of a Saturday reassembling the bookcase, reshelving the books, and comforting the dog. This accident is what precipitated Brian's call to me. A voracious reader and an even hungrier book-buyer, Brian is what author Tom Raabe comically calls a "biblioholic" – someone with an insatiable appetite to own books.

I had not slept well the night before meeting with Brian, and I was feeling pretty sleepy when we got together to organize his books. Standing in the middle of his apartment reminded me of Howe Caverns in upstate New York which I visited as a child. Stalactites and stalagmites grew in the great cave so dense that in some spots, you had to squeeze your body through small openings to traverse the cave. I distinctly remember the feeling of not wanting to move too far left or too far right for fear of bumping into one of these ancient icicles and sending it crashing to the cave floor. I had the same feeling in Brian's apartment. Books are piled so high and in such density that an elbow in the wrong direction might start a domino effect sending all the books crashing to the floor.

It is no secret that often what holds people back from discarding things is a kind of personification of them, a sort of endowment of possessions with human characteristics. It is not unusual for someone to refer to a sweater as "an old friend," for example. Books are particularly personal to their owners. The more personal, the higher the need to keep them.

Brian wants me to help him get rid of some books. When I arrive, I really have no plan. In fact, as tired as I am, I consider telling Brian perhaps we should reschedule, but I decide to go ahead. So I begin, as I often do, with the classic question, "Do you need this?" as I point randomly to a book and squelch a yawn. In my fatigue, however, the question comes out as "Does this need you?"

Brian looks up at me and laughs. "Well, that is a new approach! I'll have to think about that one for a minute. I guess now that I think about it, no, this book does not need me. We can give this one away." I was stunned. Quite by accident I had stumbled onto what later proves to be an effective method for helping people part with their high need things.

"Does this need you?" turns the principle of personification on its head. It assumes that the thing has a need for the owner rather than that the owner has a need for the thing. Accentuating this bit of ridiculousness with the question "Does this need you?" gives Brian a handle on sorting through his books. It acknowledges that the books and Brian go back a long way together, that Brian and his books have a relationship. But relationships change, break up, and sometimes end. "Does this need you?" allows Brian to acknowledge that his relationship to some of his books has changed.

Brian stands on a stool and book by book says out loud either "This needs me" or "This does not need me," like a lovelorn boy plucking the petals of a flower while saying, "She loves me, she loves me not." The "needs me" books stay shelved. The "does not need me" books are handed down to me. I pack them neatly in cartons. With Brian's permission, I donate these to Literacy Volunteers and give him the receipt so that he can deduct the donation from his taxes.

Brian's chronic book-buying will recur unless we develop an anti-book-buying strategy. We use the In/Out tactic. He can buy as many books as he wants, but for each one he buys, one must be donated, given to friends, or discarded.

Brian begins to identify books to donate to Literacy Volunteers. We call these the ransom books. I convince Brian to stash the ransom books in the basement. This clears space in his apartment. Then, each time Brian purchases a new book, he gives up one of his ransom books.

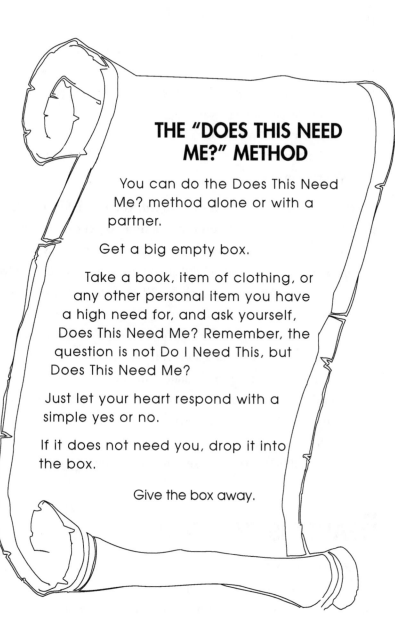

THE "DOES THIS NEED ME?" METHOD

You can do the Does This Need Me? method alone or with a partner.

Get a big empty box.

Take a book, item of clothing, or any other personal item you have a high need for, and ask yourself, Does This Need Me? Remember, the question is not Do I Need This, but Does This Need Me?

Just let your heart respond with a simple yes or no.

If it does not need you, drop it into the box.

Give the box away.

Use a Signal

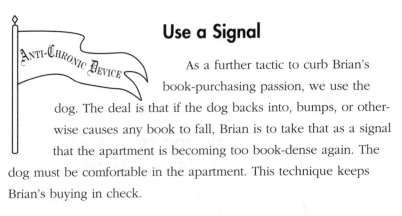

As a further tactic to curb Brian's book-purchasing passion, we use the dog. The deal is that if the dog backs into, bumps, or otherwise causes any book to fall, Brian is to take that as a signal that the apartment is becoming too book-dense again. The dog must be comfortable in the apartment. This technique keeps Brian's buying in check.

If you are chronically disorganized, you'll need a signal, something that will alert you that it's time to get organized. Conventional signals like stacks and piles and clutter usually don't hit the emotional spot. I recommend that you use signals which revolve around someone else's level of comfort or aesthetics other than your own. In Brian's case, we use the dog's comfort level. One chronically disorganized person I know uses his four year old daughter as a signal. When she cannot find a spot in his home office to color in her coloring book it's time to de-clutter. Another knows it's time to organize by simply inviting guests over once per month. Though she is not particularly put off by her own cluttered surroundings, she realizes her guests might be, and so her planned monthly dinner party is her built-in signal to make some organizing moves.

BEAUTY IS THE BEAST

Conventional wisdom insists that to be organized, you must answer the age-old question of utility. You have to ask yourself whether something is useful or not. If it is useful, keep it. If it is no longer useful, out it goes. Simple. Logical. And beyond the pale for those who organize unconventionally. It's not that chronically disorganized people cannot pose the utility question to themselves. They can. Where things break down is in the logic of the next step – the equation that says useful = keep and not useful = discard. As logical as utility may seem, it is often not a motivator for keeping or not keeping something. Sometimes a more emotional motivation is needed.

Ada is the wife of a retired university president, and a longtime civic leader in her own right. Close to the age of eighty, and a prominent public figure all her life, Ada has large collections of correspondence from far-flung friends, menus from exotic restaurants, and lists of well-to-do contributors to many a fund-raising campaign. These collections occupy a good deal of living space in Ada's lovely home. They are scattered about on all surfaces including her bed. In addition, Ada has collected hundreds of newspaper columns and magazine articles reflecting her wide range of interests and her life-long commitment to learning. These have totally overrun the guest room and other areas of the house.

"I used to think of these as treasures," her soft voice begins on my answering machine; "but now they're just junk!" it ends with a thundering voice so loud I can scarcely believe it is the same person. I call Ada back immediately, because I must confess my true desire is to meet this fascinating woman.

Once settled into her parlor, we begin to sift through a representative stack of papers. This is a helpful procedure that gives me clues as to how a person with major quantities of papers might be swayed to part with some. I note that whenever Ada comes across a magazine article she will tell me how dear the person is who sent it to her, but she never comments on the content of the article itself. Ada expresses how impressed she is with the unique turn of phrase in a newspaper column, but she professes no need for the information contained in the column itself. She saves a letter because of the stationery it is printed on, rather than because of anything the letter says.

It occurs to me that beauty and not utility underlies Ada's saving habit. Ada would no sooner part with something of beauty than a child her blankee. The key is to use Ada's good taste and adoration of beauty to loosen her grip on things. I remembered her phone message – "...they used to be treasures...but now they're junk." Instead of asking Ada the utility-laden question, "Will you ever use this?" I change my tactics and propose that we go on a treasure hunt.

TREASURE HUNTING

Ada likes the idea. Like a miner searching for gems, she proficiently sorts through her documents and possessions, quickly differentiating the treasures from the non-treasures. Those things that do not make "the treasure cut" are either discarded or put aside to be given away. **The positive act of searching for treasures is a more effective organizing method than the negative act of throwing junk away.** We keep the treasures, of course, and find beautiful ways to contain them. Exotic menus are stored inside ornate hatboxes. The lid opens on a hand-embroidered hassock where we store Ada's correspondences. Inside an embossed, leather suitcase we put travel articles. Clippings about gardening are tucked into plastic baggies and placed inside clay planter pots in the mud room. It does not concern Ada to be able to retrieve or use any of these items. She means only to have them, or, more precisely, to treasure them.

Use Non-Family To Keep You Organized

Ada's tendency to accumulate things of beauty is constant. She cannot control it by herself. So she and I have arranged to go treasure hunting three times per year. You can go treasure hunting with anyone, but Ada prefers using me to her family or friends because, as a professional organizer, I am objective. Ada feels judged by her family and friends. Her daughter once told her, "Mom, I know these placemats are very pretty, but you never use them. Give them away!" Ada promised she would but as soon as her daughter left, she decided to treasure them. A professional organizer is non-judgmental, and that makes a big difference to people who are chronically disorganized and so often criticized by family and friends.

As an additional measure I have arranged for an intern from the local historical society to visit with Ada after she and I finish each treasure hunt. We assemble boxes of materials that might have historical value but are not treasures. The intern picks up these boxes and then the historical society does its own version of treasure hunting.

Recently, Ada and I attended an exhibit at the historical society on the history of a local Atlanta college. Ada's husband was its first president. Among the items on display was Ada's menu from the first racially integrated faculty luncheon.

Build a Shrine

I read about shrines in a *National Geographic* article about Mexico. Shrines are typically built to honor the memory of the dead, but shrines can also be built to acknowledge loss. For example, Ross is a retired teacher. A lot of the clutter in his home has to do with his long career as a teacher. Ross loved being a teacher. Recently retired, he is still active in a professional association of teachers and likes to keep up to date on trends in the field. Ross has found it exceptionally difficult to dispose of anything related to his previous teaching career.

He has saved students' projects; magazine articles about teaching methods; pedagogical materials like teaching games and other aids; all his continuing education certificates, seminar notes,...even obituaries of teachers that he has admired. His lifetime habit of keeping everything related to teaching is now pushing out room for anything else in his life.

Ross and I built a shrine to his teaching career. On a small, pretty, wooden table we placed a framed photo of Ross receiving a teaching award. Next to that we scrolled up a copy of his original teaching certificate and tied it with a bright ribbon. A collector's copy of *Teacher's Magazine* is proudly displayed on the table next to another photo of Ross with his last students. A few gifts received from students over the years and Ross' favorite pen for marking papers (red, of course) complete the shrine. Every day Ross is able to remember his contribution to the teaching profession by the daily viewing of his shrine, and he has thrown away all the other memorabilia.

KINETIC SYMPATHY

Radical organizing methods which incorporate, and even exaggerate, emotions can help chronically disorganized people organize their papers and possessions, get rid of excess, and maintain organizing success, especially in instances where logic-based conventional systems have failed. Perhaps no discovery about chronic disorganization seems more counter-logical than kinetic sympathy. **Kinetic sympathy is the art of organizing without the act of touching.** I discovered it quite by accident while working with Janette.

I met Janette at a "Women and Health Care" networking event. At the event, we are all asked to introduce ourselves and say a bit about what we do. I give my "professional organizer" spiel and sit down. Janette introduces herself as a nurse of over twenty years, intensely committed to improving the health of women. "I'm a packrat...can't throw anything away," she whispers to me as she takes her seat. "Right up my alley," I whisper back. Janette and I arrange to meet at her apartment to discuss her organizing situation.

Janette's apartment is decorated in classic chronic style. Clothing that cannot be stuffed into overcrowded closets is heaped on the couch. Magazines, mail, and the ubiquitous mail order catalogues cover every table and surface. Knickknacks of all kinds abound. Little porcelain thimbles, ceramic plates, and seashells crowd small shelves, cupboards, and end tables. Larger shelves and hutches hold dolls, record albums, and miscellaneous dinnerware pieces. The credenza, sideboard, and china cabinets conceal tools, light bulbs, and a grand assortment of gadgets of all kinds. "I told you I never throw anything away," Janette reminds me, half embarrassed, half defensive.

I am always a little confused in such circumstances. On the one hand, I respect Janette's commitment to get organized, and tell her, "I know my being here means you want to do something different to get organized. I just want you to know I respect you for that decision."

But, on the other hand, Janette sounds as if she has a policy of not throwing anything away. So I ask her, "If you do not plan to throw anything out, and yet I am here, well, I'm a little confused about how I can help."

"I'm about to be evicted," Janette confesses. "My landlord thinks my stuff is injurious to his apartment, which of course it isn't! He really cannot make me leave because I have a lease, but it is up in four months and I don't want him to have any reason not to renew it."

Janette begins to cry.

I sit down beside her. She weeps and I give her tissues. consolation and time. Slowly she comes around and I assure her that we will make progress (though I am sure conventional organizing will not work). Between us I open a large black plastic bag, the heavy duty kind used for leaves and twigs. I inhale deeply. Janette inhales deeply. I exhale deeply. Janette exhales deeply.

We begin. Reaching over to the couch I take a skirt from it and hold it up for her inspection. "Out," she says unequivocally and, considering myself lucky, I toss the skirt into the garbage bag. I hold up a blouse. "Maybe," she says, and I put it aside. I take a belt from the couch and hand it to Janette. Hardly looking at it at all, she announces, "Keep," and puts the belt beside her on the couch. I hold up another blouse. "Out," she responds, and I plop it into the bag. Janette picks up a skirt from the couch and decides to keep it.

A pattern begins to emerge. Whenever **I** hold up a piece of clothing, Janette is apt to discard it or at least give it a "maybe". Whenever **she** touches the clothing, she keeps it without exception. If I can manage to "feed" her each item to see, but not to touch, we have a chance of her deciding it can be disposed of. Once Janette touches it, there is no chance of disposal at all.

Coincidence? Maybe, but no other pattern emerges. Some of the "Keep" clothes are damaged, old, and worthless but, having touched them, she keeps them. Some of the "Out" clothes are in better shape than the "Keep" items but, not having touched them, she throws most of them away.

I call this phenomenon "kinetic sympathy." Lacking formal training in psychology, I am at a loss to explain it, but it is clear that touching a thing can set off an emotional response for chronically disorganized people. Perhaps the touching of a thing changes a simple act of throwing out into an emotional act of letting go. I really do not know.

The idea of generating kinetic sympathy is not a new one. Car salesmen use it all the time. When I shopped for my first new car, I came into the dealership determined to talk price, financing, and safety. The salesman, on the other hand, had only one goal – to get me seated behind the wheel of the car I liked. He knew that once I sat in that comfy driver's seat and wrapped my hands around the slick leather steering wheel I would be hooked. And he was right. Sitting there in that new car, I was already calculating how much more per month I might be able to swing to own that baby.

In this instance, I am a victim of kinetic sympathy. Some types of therapeutic massage are based on emotional responses to touch, a kind of kinetic sympathy. And we witness kinetic sympathy when we see relatives who have not been on speaking terms with one another for long periods of time embrace at a funeral, marriage, or other family gathering, and suddenly cry and forgive one another.

And so it is with Janette. Just as I cannot resist the car I have touched, Janette cannot resist keeping everything she touches.

Janette and I establish a rule to counteract kinetic sympathy. During our organizing session, she may point to, comment upon, and look at the things she and I are sorting, *but she cannot touch them*. With this rule in place, we are able to make progress.

Janette's invisible field of possession, her kinetic sympathy, is overcome by denying her the ability to touch things. Using this technique; Friends, Acquaintances, and Strangers; and the In/Out negotiations discussed previously, the clutter in Janette's apartment recedes and the landlord begs off. Still, Janette is highly susceptible to re-cluttering and so further steps are necessary.

Cut Clutter at the Source

Anti-Chronic Device

The primary sources of Janette's over-collecting are flea markets and garage sales. Flea markets and garage sales are overpowering to most chronically disorganized people. In fact, people who are well-organized are known to "lose it" at such venues. I recall two elderly sisters who lived together and wanted to reduce the clutter in their home. One sister neatly arranged objects for a garage sale on one side of the driveway. The second sister did the same with her stuff on the opposite side of the driveway. Pretty soon, the first sister drifted over to the items of the second sister and found herself buying most of them. Meanwhile, the second sister journeyed over to the other side of the driveway and eventually bought up most of her sister's goods. They simply exchanged each other's stuff! Such is the power of garage sales.

To maintain organizing success, Janette must limit her flea market and garage sale outings to one per month. She must attend them with a buddy. Janette can point to an item she is interested in, but the buddy picks it up for Janette's closer inspection. Janette keeps her hands in her pockets. In this way, she purchases much less than she used to.

CHAPTER
3

LEARNING AND
ORGANIZING STYLES

Learning style refers to the dominate way you perceive and process information. Years ago, it was believed that all children learned exactly the same way. Later it was discovered that all children do not learn the same way, even when everything else is equal (intelligence, age, same teacher, same class material). Many reasons can account for these differences in learning, but one reason turns out to be differences in the learning style of the child.

There are three types of learning styles, defined as: auditory, learning through hearing; visual, learning through seeing; and kinesthetic, learning through moving and touching. Capitalizing on a person's learning style dominance (or compensating for a learning style weakness) can greatly influence learning. For example, children who are strong visual learners and not good auditory learners may not learn to read well with a teacher who only reads material out loud but doesn't point to words on a blackboard. Learning style dominance is not as clear-cut as other neurological dominances, like being left-handed or right-handed, but a diversity of learning styles clearly does exist.

Because organizing, like reading, is a learned activity, it reflects our learning style. The problem is that conventional organizing methods, for the most part, fail to appreciate learning style differences. Show me a person who tries to use organizing systems that are incompatible with her learning style, and I'll show you a person who is chronically disorganized.

THE AUDITORY OFFICE

There is a little joke around the Department about Beth's office. It's known as the Bermuda Triangle. Even Jamela, Beth's secretary, calls it that. "I send things in there, but nothing ever comes out!" Jamela quips. Beth's office is heaped high with stacks of paper on all surfaces. The telltale disappearing desk, a hallmark of chronic disorganization, is evident and, of course, the floor stacks are a dead giveaway. Beth is being promoted and Jamela is going with her up the corporate ladder. Beth will have a new supervisor who is a real stickler about messy offices, so Beth and Jamela have decided to call me. With Beth's consent, I decide that an interview with Jamela might give me insight into how Beth works. After all, Jamela is on the "front-line," as it were, and knows how Beth operates.

Jamela tells me that Beth is an excellent facilitator. No one is better than Beth at running meetings. Beth can move an agenda along, encourage discussion, and keep everyone on the topic at hand. But more amazingly, Beth remembers the content of the meeting verbatim with hardly any notes at all. "Last week I asked Beth if she wanted to buy a gift for Ron, the receptionist, who will turn 50. She said, 'In May of last year, we took a vote at a Department meeting and decided that instead of gifts we would send a donation to the charity of choice of the person having a birthday. Send Ron a birthday card, and ask him what charity he wants us to send a check to.' Beth can even recall how each person voted on this policy!" Jamela adds.

On the telephone Beth can run off facts and figures, make decisions on the spot, and take charge. She's a dynamo, but once she's in her office, seated in front of a stack of papers to attend to, she shuts down. Jamela says she cannot count on Beth to read, sign, or make a decision on any document she puts in her office.

"Once it goes into the Bermuda Triangle I can pretty much assume I will never see it again. The words I dread most around here are 'Leave it on my desk.' Right away I know I'm doomed. I end up making copies of everything I give to Beth so I can keep track of things. That just doubles the amount of paper around here and ties my time up at the copy machine."

"I think Beth is an auditory person," I offer.

"What does that mean?"

"She is strong at meetings and on the phone, and has a great verbal memory. These are clues to an auditory person. It means you have to operate the office and do your work using the spoken word more than the written word. For instance, instead of sending memos and other written communications into Beth's office, you'll need to talk to each other more. I think what has to drive this office is not documentation, but conversation."

I recommend that Jamela and Beth meet several times a day. They both look at me in disbelief. Surely I can't mean it. Meet several times a day? Who's got that kind of time?

"If you spend just fifteen minutes first thing in the morning, five minutes after lunch, and ten minutes at about three o'clock, you can discuss the progress and status of existing work, troubleshoot, and reprioritize work if necessary. In what will amount to thirty minutes a day, you will accomplish more than any amount of memos and notes exchanged between you...And meet standing up," I add. "How's that?" Jamela asks. "Stand up," I repeat. "It will keep the meetings brief and very focused. Don't sit down."

To bolster my case I tell Beth and Jamela about Paul, a client of mine who is blind. Because he cannot see, Paul and his secretary meet several times a day to go over work verbally. They leave messages for each other on voice mail. They use speaking instead of writing as the primary means of communication because of Paul's disability.

In no way do I mean to imply that Beth is disabled; but why not use the learning style she is most comfortable with? Beth communicates verbally and processes information auditorily.

Jamela and I begin the process of reorganizing Beth's office on the basis of her auditory strengths. We use a microcassette recorder, one of those mini–tape recorders that you hold in your hand. As Jamela picks up a long-neglected document from Beth's desk, she dictates a message to Beth like: "Document A is a memo from a client requesting a meeting. Please advise me whether I should set this meeting up. Document B is a report sent back from headquarters requesting more in-depth research. Shall I do the Internet research or do you want to handle this?" and so on. Jamela transforms all the reports, notes, memos, and other written communications on the desk into auditory messages.

Beth, for her part, will put on headphones (she loves headphones) and listen to Jamela's recording while referring to the appropriate document. She will either respond to Jamela in one of their short, stand-up meetings or, will speak with Jamela over the intercom. Frankly, Jamela finds Beth's frequent use of the intercom distracting to her own work, but the tape recordings and intercom put fast closure on their work so she has learned to tolerate it. Jamela also leaves voice mail rather than e-mail messages.

Beth and Jamela have been using their auditory office successfully for three months now. They have made some modifications. They still have stand-up meetings during the day but they have added a longer, strategic meeting mid-month. Beth has also installed a compact disk player in her office. At home, classical music playing softly in the background helped her concentrate on household chores like paying bills and cooking. "Even if I turn the TV on and don't watch it, the background noise helps me focus," she explains. So she also listens to music while she works in her office.

"The paperless office is about as likely as the paperless bathroom," notes the *Wall Street Journal*. It would be idealistic to think that Beth and Jamela could convert everything in the office from a visual, paper-bound, written medium into an auditory one. But, if you learn better through your ears than your eyes you will find the following list of auditory organizing tools valuable.

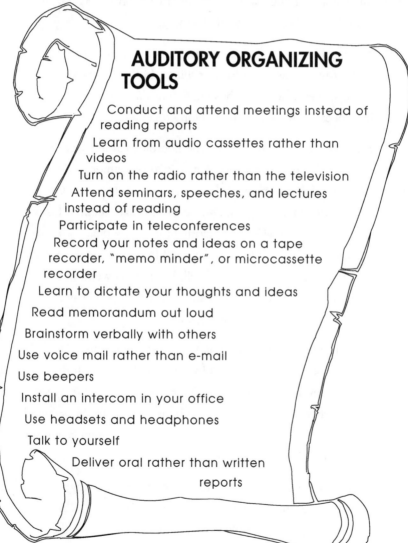

AUDITORY ORGANIZING TOOLS

Conduct and attend meetings instead of reading reports

Learn from audio cassettes rather than videos

Turn on the radio rather than the television

Attend seminars, speeches, and lectures instead of reading

Participate in teleconferences

Record your notes and ideas on a tape recorder, "memo minder", or microcassette recorder

Learn to dictate your thoughts and ideas

Read memorandum out loud

Brainstorm verbally with others

Use voice mail rather than e-mail

Use beepers

Install an intercom in your office

Use headsets and headphones

Talk to yourself

Deliver oral rather than written reports

FISHING IN THE GARAGE

Oscar is not chronically disorganized in the classical sense. The onset of his severe disorganization is fairly recent, the result of a motorcycle accident that left him neurologically impaired in certain fundamental and strange ways. He cannot categorize. Organizing Oscar taught me about kinesthetic learning.

The catechism of categories reigns supreme in our society. Nearly all of us can associate similar things, both visually and mentally. We can then categorize these like-things and even subcategorize them because we know they belong together.

Oscar has no categories at all. The neurological impairment resulting from his motorcycle accident wiped out, among other capacities, his ability to mentally group like-things together. Oscar can stare at two similar objects, and never associate them in his mind as alike. Pam, Oscar's wife, is a charming, patient woman who loves her husband very much. Oscar nearly died in the accident, so Pam is grateful just to have him alive and well, despite his weird neurological wiring. Not one to complain, Pam is, however, at her wit's end trying to find a way to get Oscar organized.

"If I put things away in small jars or plastic containers, Oscar has a devil of a time finding what he's looking for. It's easier for him to just rummage around on the garage floor. It's not that he can't see. It's just that when he pictures the item he is looking for in his mind, he can't translate it into the real thing in containers. Rummaging on the floor is the only thing that works."

Oscar must rummage. He has to use touching as a way to verify what he seeks, because his mind cannot verify for him. Oscar spreads out all his tools, supplies, nails and screws all over the garage floor.

"We really need to pull the car and the kids' bicycles inside the garage. And with winter coming, it sure would be nice to pull the lawn mower in too. Got any ideas?" Pam asks politely.

This is my kind of organizing job. Tough, unorthodox, and just a little bit desperate. But even with that kind of challenge I have no workable ideas right off the bat. "Where is Oscar?" I ask. "Away on a fishing trip. He said he probably would be in the way, so we planned for you to come while he is away fishing."

Fishing. Fishing. The words roll around in my head. I spy in the corner of the garage some fishing gear – high boots, a couple of fishing rods, an old tackle box, and fishnet. "We could put a fishnet down on the garage floor, pile all the stuff into it, and hoist all this stuff to the ceiling,"I say unconvincingly.

"Pardon?" Pam replies. (When a Southerner says Pardon to you it is not just a neutral sign that you were not heard. "Pardon" really means they think you are a little bit nuts and you are being given one more chance to redeem yourself.)

"I think we should put a fishnet down on the floor, hook it up to pulleys, and hoist all this stuff up to the ceiling," I explain. Pam looks at me for a long time. She slowly looks up at the ceiling, then she looks down at the garage floor as if putting all the elements together in her mind. "Okay," she says hesitantly, "but how?"

"Oscar will need to help."

Oscar calls me when he returns from his trip. "I heard about your idea. I don't know what to say. It's so odd. But, then so am I so maybe it will work. The fishnet I have is a very loose weave. I'll pick up a tight weave one, pulleys, pulley cord – the whole ball of wax from the hardware store. Can you meet me on Saturday?"

"Sure. But, Oscar, to be honest with you, I have never done this before."

"What? You've never gone fishing in a garage before?", he says kiddingly.

Pam uses a magnet to collect all the little nails and screws that might fall through the fishnet. We dump these into wide, round, shallow pie plates and set them on the workbench. The pie plates spread the tiny items around so Oscar can rummage through them easily.

Pam and I remove everything heavy from the garage floor. A hand-drill, a can of paint, a thick roll of wire, for instance, are just too dangerous to pull aloft. "One head trauma in the house at a time is plenty, thank you very much," Pam cautions. Meanwhile, Oscar does his thing. He drills holes to mount the pulleys, runs cord through the netting and down through the pulleys.

As the kids and curious neighbors look on, Oscar instructs Pam and me to lay the netting down on the floor. We pile all the stuff from the garage floor onto it, and, with Pam on one pulley and me across from her on the other, at the count of three Oscar directs us to slowly tug the pulley cords. The onlookers hold their collective breath. The net rises slowly from the floor. Pam's side sags. Oscar tells her to pull a little harder. The net corrects itself, then sags dangerously over to my side. The crowd lets out a loud "Ohhhhhh...." Oscar yells "Stop!" He bats the underside of the netting a little, it straightens out, and we continue pulling.

Finally the net rises close to the garage ceiling. We secure the pulleys. We look up at what appears to be a lumpy giant asleep in a hammock twelve feet above the garage floor. The crowd goes wild. They applaud and whistle as Pam drives the car into the garage.

When Oscar needs to rummage he simply pulls the car out and lowers the net. Since most of his fix-it projects are done on the weekend when the car is out of the garage anyway there are hardly any problems lowering the net.

We find other ways to optimize Oscar's use of touch in an effort to get him organized. We paint a wall-sized pegboard black. Oscar carefully holds a drill up to the pegboard and outlines it with white chalk. We mount the drill on the pegboard inside the outline. Each time the drill needs to be replaced on the pegboard, Oscar holds the tool up to the pegboard and matches its profile with the outline. In this way he is able to remount all his tools.

When we have organized the garage as best we can on a kinesthetic-basis, Oscar and Pam try it out for several months. They invite me to return to see their many modifications. The pulley system is redesigned to be workable by one person instead two. The black pegboard is for frequently used tools only. A smaller, red pegboard for less-frequently used tools is added. Thus, Oscar can use the colors black and red to aid him in finding his tools. The giant, though slimmer, still sleeps overhead in a hammock.

Verbing Victor

It started out as a harmless April Fool's joke. To Victor's co-workers it is a mystery how someone so productive and so neat in appearance as Victor can keep his desk so cluttered with papers that they can barely see him when he's seated. Victor's co-workers think it might be funny to report him to the fire department as a fire hazard. And it is funny...for a little while. Victor receives the fire hazard citation from the fireman with a good-hearted laugh and jokes about his disorganization as much as everyone else. When the office quiets down Victor closes his office door and phones me.

Action-oriented phrases pepper Victor's speech. "I feel like I can't hold on any longer. If I don't come to grips with my disorganization, I'm going to go under." In their book, ***Quantum Learning: Unleashing the Genius in You***, Bobbi DePorter and Mike Hernacki suggest that one clue to a kinesthetic learner is how action words fill their language. Victor fits the bill perfectly.

Also, when I meet with Victor he is unable to sit down for any length of time. He'll sit in his chair only long enough to spring out of it again in an instant. He tends to walk around the office while he speaks, and if he does sit, he can be counted on to twirl a pen in his hand or, in some other small way, create motion. So I get the impression that Victor might have kinesthetic leanings.

"Pick up a piece of paper and say the first action verb that comes to mind", I suggest.

"Call," Victor asserts as he hands me a piece of paper with the efficiency of a machine. "Write," he commands as the next sheet is given to me. "Read" is the fate of a third document. And so we continue, ascribing verbs to all the documents. I attach a sticky note to each piece of paper indicating the verb. Victor begins to remind me of the Queen at the croquet game in *Alice in Wonderland*. He royally proclaims verbs for this and that paper while I trot behind him. When we come to a paper or document that is trash, I half expect him to say "Off with its head" but the verb "Toss" is as close as we get. Like all good kings and queens, Victor makes up the rules for the Verbing Game as we go along. He outlaws the verbs Do, Decide, and Review. "Too wimpy. Too evasive. Give me strong action verbs!", Victor demands.

Every piece of paper in his office is tagged with a sticky note with a verb on it. We gather all those marked Copy and place them by the copy machine. Next to the couch in his office we place all the documents tagged Read. Those marked Order, Subscribe, and Pay are placed together on one side of the desk near the checkbook, with Pay on top. Call is put by the telephone; Mail by the postage meter.

These classical verbs are joined by the trendy verbs of the late '90s. These new verbs are tricky because they double as nouns. "Fax", for example, used to be a noun referring to the name of a machine that could miraculously transmit documents over a telephone line. Now Fax is a very big verb. Database is a noun in its own right. But Victor's "Database" refers to the action he must take to organize his business cards and returned mail. On a later visit, I encourage Victor to use some unconventional verbs. "Digest" can be substituted for "Review" and "Clone" is more fun than "Copy." I have a client who uses "Strive" instead of "Plan" and "Holler" (very Southern) instead of "Call". Unconventional verbs are more fun and so, more memorable.

To build on Victor's kinesthetic nature, we also designate mini-action centers in his office. His Mail Center, for example, includes all his outgoing mail and all the supplies he could possibly need to carry out that action: stamps, postage meter, envelopes, a scale, etc. The credenza becomes the Call Center. We move Victor's phone off his desk and on to the credenza behind him. The Call documents, his Rolodex^{TM}, long distance phone log, Yellow Pages, and many pads are placed at the Call Center.

There are typically over 3,000 loose pieces of paper in the office of an average chronically disorganized person, a fact well appreciated by Victor's co-workers. They are so impressed with his improved office that they present him with a check (real) to pay for the (fake) fire hazard citation.

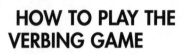

HOW TO PLAY THE VERBING GAME

Walk through your office

Pick up a piece of paper and assign an action verb to it. Ask yourself "What is the next action step I need to take with this paper?"

Write the verb on a sticky note and affix it to the paper

Verb every single piece of paper you encounter

Group the papers by like-verbs

Create mini-action centers or put the verbed papers where the action will take place

SAMPLE ACTION VERBS

Call	Correspond	Pay
Read	File	Mail
Order	Subscribe	Sign
Copy	Distribute	Delegate

UNCONVENTIONAL VERBS

Enjoy	Share	Improve
Strive	Create	Solve
Clone	Direct	Digest
Invent	Originate	Launch
Renew	Strengthen	Teach

UNHELPFUL VERBS

Complete	Do	Decide
Prepare	Review	Plan

The Paper Police

Victor's chronic disorganization is a tendency he will always have to counteract. He verbs papers all day long, but, for good measure, he walks his office at the end of each day. He deliberately looks for papers misplaced or untagged. He visits each mini-center and sees that each is properly stocked. He makes a point of touching each squared-off, neat stack of verbed papers. "I feel a little like a policeman with a nightstick checking for crime. I'm not sure why I have to touch each stack. It makes me feel like I've been thorough, like affixing a seal of approval."

KINESTHETIC TIME MANAGEMENT

This positive response to things kinesthetic by some chronically disorganized people has application in physical environments, like the office or the home. The organizing activity we call time management is made up less of physical elements, like papers and files and possessions, than it is comprised of conceptual processes, like planning and prioritizing. But kinesthetics can also help a chronically disorganized person manage time.

Conventional organizing insists that the conditions under which we plan and prioritize require a lack of distraction. But I have met many chronically disorganized people who thrive on commotion and distraction, at least at tolerable levels. I believe this positive response to commotion is related to the issue of kinesthetics. It sounds counter-logical that some people can concentrate and perform time management tasks better when surrounded by commotion and clamor than peace and quiet. But you have not yet heard Iris' story.

CAFETERIA CONCENTRATION

Iris owns a head-hunting firm, an extremely competitive industry in Atlanta. Iris and I do time management sessions designed to help her achieve business and personal goals. On our first appointment at Iris' office, I notice that she has difficulty concentrating. She cannot keep her mind on the task at hand. Every six minutes or so she jumps up from her desk and goes off to get a drink of water, make a phone call, or walk down the hall to speak to someone. It is as if she needs to take frequent little breaks in order to keep going at all.

In an effort to make our time management sessions more productive, I suggest that, next time, we meet at Morrison's, a busy Atlanta cafeteria-style restaurant where I have noted many individuals sitting alone at tables doing paperwork.

"You want me to meet you at Morrison's?" Iris says incredulously. "Are you sure you don't want to go someplace a little better?"

"It's really not the food I'm after. It's the environment. But they do have great okra."

What I have in mind here is an idea I learned from a colleague who works with adults with Attention Deficit Disorder (ADD). ADD is a neurobiological disability that interferes with a person's ability to sustain attention or focus on a task. Sometimes it also involves difficulty in delaying impulsive behavior.

Apparently, one of the most distracting stimulus ADD people encounter is often not *external* noise, but *internal* "noise". Internal noise includes extraneous ideas, tangential thoughts, and mental to-do lists. It is this internal noise that frequently distracts a person from the task at hand.

If external noise can be turned up a notch, so the theory goes, internal noise can settle down. Of course, the external noise and commotion cannot be too loud or too distracting or else the balancing act between external and internal noise is thrown off. The external commotion of a cafeteria can be just enough to cancel out internal noise.

The commotion at Morrison's is pretty intense, and I fear I have made a mistake. The staff moves about carrying clattering dishes; patrons file by on the cafeteria line; people talk loudly while seated on chairs with casters that seem always to be sliding about; and kids run about freely. Everything seems slightly in motion. Iris and I sit with pecan pie and sweet iced tea (the only kind you'll find in the South) and settle down to work.

I do not know if Iris has ADD. We have never discussed it. But I do know that at Morrison's Iris is very focused. She spreads her planner, calendar, and pad out on the table in front of her, and we work for nearly one hour time managing her schedule for the next three months. Iris does not get up from the table once (though she does frequently sip water).

"Oh my goodness, look at the time!" she exclaims. "I can't believe we've been here an hour and I haven't checked in with my office." She pulls out her cell phone and makes a quick call. When she is finished, she comments, "You were right. I can concentrate better here than at the office. Something about the busyness, the swirl of things going on around me is more conducive to thinking than the nice, quiet solitude of my office."

This preference for commotion is very strong with some chronically disorganized people. Myra blesses the day that boutique coffee shops found a market in Atlanta. Once a week, she tosses her bills and unopened mail in a big sack and heads for the coffee shop in her neighborhood. With double-latte in hand and surrounded by busy coffee-drinkers, Myra knocks off her mail and pays all her bills, something she cannot accomplish at home. I myself find that I am extremely productive in airports and often get more done waiting for the next available flight than working in my office. I believe commotion, noise, and motion speak to a kinesthetic side of chronically disorganized people who struggle with time management.

Breaking out of to-do prison

Michael's home looks like something out of **Better Homes and Gardens** and his office is well-organized – not a stray piece of paper in sight. But Michael is chronically disorganized. How can this be? Michael has been waging a war with time management for the better part of his life. His days are filled with stress and conflict because "I cannot get my hands around time", as Michael puts it. He has tried and failed many times. "Time is so abstract. It's not like you can touch time like you can paper or clutter". Maybe. Or maybe so.

"Here", Michael says as a large wad of pads lands on his desk with that distinctive thud only legal pads can make. "These are my to-do lists."

Yellow lined pads with sheet after sheet of entries greet me. Some entries are crossed through with hearty lines, while others are circled round and round for accentuation. The pads bulge from rumpled pages and dog-eared corners. Many entries repeat on subsequent papers, carried over like a recurring toothache.

While I study these pads, Michael pulls out yet another clump of pads. "I thought if I used shorter pads I might actually get to the end of a to-do list. So I had these printed up," Michael explains. These shorter pads have "Michael's To Do List" custom printed across the top. "It didn't work. Though the pads are shorter, I still never reach the end."

"Three months ago I attended a time management seminar which set me back $559.00 – not including the cost of the dayplanner and audio tapes I bought. Here I am at a time management seminar and all I can think about is how much time it is taking up! It wasn't totally useless though. I picked up a few good tips and I bought this." Michael says as he whirls around in his desk chair and chest-presses a hefty dayplanner from his credenza. He heaves it on the desk where it is added to the pyre of pads and lists already piled up.

"This planner has six sections, weighs in at two pounds, and I have spent more time with it than my wife!", Michael complains. "I kept it up for about three weeks. I still feel overwhelmed all the time. I can never seem to stay on top of things, let alone plan ahead. I'm totally stressed out. It's like time is something I can't control."

In my mind's eye I envision the lines on Michael's to-do pads running vertically instead of horizontally so that they resemble the bars of a prison cell. Michael is a cartoon stick figure behind the prison bars clutching them like a prisoner. It occurs to me that *it is not just the content of Michael's lists that is problematic, but it is that he makes lists at all.* I believe the lists themselves contribute to Michael's time management problems.

Michael's time management systems all share one characteristic; they are one-dimensional, stagnant systems. The lined pads, the to-do lists, and the dayplanner all capture tasks and freeze them onto paper. But Michael's *life* is very dynamic. His priorities are always changing and his learning style is kinesthetic. The conventional time management tools he uses seem ill-suited. I propose that we abandon the planner and to-do lists altogether. "Let's find a way for you to touch time", I suggest.

I open up an unused file folder and write Now on the inside left panel and Not Now on the inside right panel. Michael and I transpose every single task from his many lists on to individual sticky notes. Michael affixes them one at a time to either the Now or the Not Now panel. They both fill up quickly so we keep the panel called Now, and retitle the Not Now panel to Very Soon. Then we add a third panel called Parking.

Once a task on the Now panel is complete, it is replaced with a sticky note from the Very Soon panel. As more and more Now tasks are completed, Very Soon stickies are moved over to take their place. If a new task needs space in Now, one Now must be downgraded to a Very Soon, otherwise that new task must wait on the Very Soon panel. Tasks that do not need to be done Now or Very Soon are stuck on the Parking panel. When a Very Soon task is completed, a task can be moved out of Parking to the Very Soon panel. In this way, tasks are always moving from Parking to Very Soon, to Now. We call this the Panel System.

From a conventional time management point of view, Now and Very Soon are ambiguous. This is exactly what appeals to Michael. Because Now and Very Soon are not calendar-oriented (i.e., they are not daily, weekly or monthly objectives) Michael likes them much better. He is unable to discipline himself to be realistic about how much he can accomplish daily or weekly, so the panels frame Michael's time physically. He simply cannot add more tasks than a panel will hold.

But the part of the Panel System Michael likes best are the sticky notes themselves. "I love being able to move them around. I can upgrade a Very Soon to a Now, or downgrade a Now to a Very Soon. I can group a bunch of stickies together or arrange them in any sequence or priority instantly...I can do whatever I want with them", Michael proclaims. This flexible, tactile element of time management is crucial to Michael. He says the Panel System lets him "touch time".

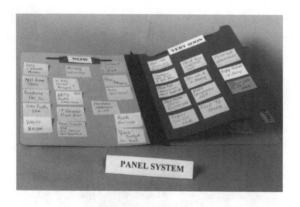

Barbara has created her own version of "touching time." She is the manager of one of Atlanta's best known (and busiest) spas. Barbara uses flash cards made from index cards to manage her tasks and her time. Each flash card has decorative stickers on it. A flash card with car stickers on it lists errands Barbara must run. A flash card with an arrow pointing down lists tasks Barbara must delegate to her staff. An arrow pointing up indicates something to discuss with the spa's owner. Barbara has a card with telephone stickers on it for calls she must make. One flash card is pink with a fire truck sticker on it. If things get particularly hectic at the spa, at least this card tells Barbara the most urgent tasks to do that day.

Barbara flips through her flash cards all day long. She adds tasks to the cards each time a task is completed. If a card gets filled up, she simply makes another one. "I like to shuffle them. I can't do that with a to-do list!", Barbara notes. I encourage her to make one more flash card. It does not list a to-do item. It symbolizes no action to take. It simply says "Barbara" on it. This is to remind Barbara to be sure to "deal herself in" every day; to make certain she does something good for herself every day.

Chronically disorganized people are notorious for underestimating how long things will take to do. It's helpful to represent tasks with kinesthetic models such as panel systems or flash cards. A client and I once even constructed a Lego™ model of a complex project!

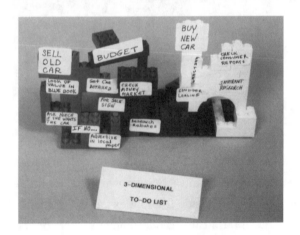

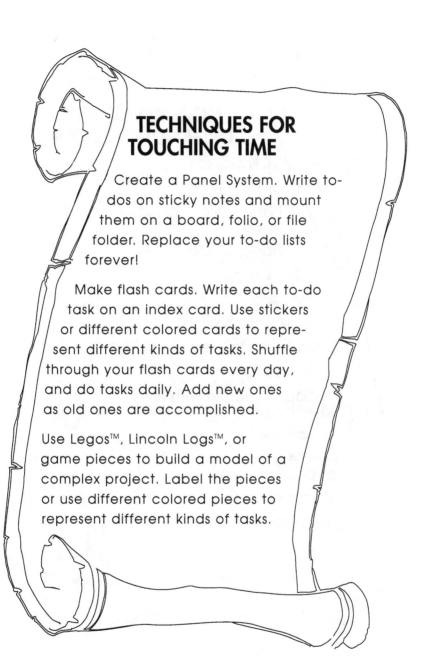

TECHNIQUES FOR TOUCHING TIME

Create a Panel System. Write to-dos on sticky notes and mount them on a board, folio, or file folder. Replace your to-do lists forever!

Make flash cards. Write each to-do task on an index card. Use stickers or different colored cards to represent different kinds of tasks. Shuffle through your flash cards every day, and do tasks daily. Add new ones as old ones are accomplished.

Use Legos™, Lincoln Logs™, or game pieces to build a model of a complex project. Label the pieces or use different colored pieces to represent different kinds of tasks.

MORE KINESTHETIC ORGANIZING TOOLS

Clipboards

Sticky Notes

Pace while thinking or rock in place

Analog clocks

Flip Charts

Models

Walk while talking

Three-ring binders

Flowcharts

Surround yourself with low-level commotion or noise

Action centers

Fondle objects (silly putty, paperclips, pens)

Chairs on casters

Doodle

Visual Organizing

We have seen how an auditory office can make the best use of a person's auditory learning style. A kinesthetic learning style can be optimized with organizing systems that are kinesthetically-oriented. The most common learning and organizing style is visual. Visual organizing is organizing through the eyes, as opposed to through the ears (auditory) or through motion or touch (kinesthetic). Visual organizing uses color, color-coding, transparency and other visual tools.

Color-coding has been popular for many years. Red, for instance, stimulates, excites, and increases heart, brain, and respiratory function. Americans respond to red as urgent. That is why red is used for stop lights and emergency vehicles. Yellow jogs the memory; a perfect choice for Post-It Notes™! Green has several meanings, including relaxation, new beginnings, and money.

Manila, the color of file folders, creates very little, if any, vibration. On machines used to measure energy output (vibrations emitted by color) manila registers nearly a flat-line. If you want to kill action on anything, putting it inside a manila folder will do the trick. Frances and I color-coded her boss!

How To Color-Code Your Boss

I remember that it was National Secretaries' Day when Frances called me. Jacob, her boss, asked Frances what she might like as a gift. Thinking she would choose a day off, dinner at a nice restaurant, or perhaps a gift certificate, Jacob was taken aback when Frances replied, "I want to get you organized!" She explained that getting her boss organized would reduce the stress of her own job and be a gift to her all year round. So Jacob gave Frances the green light to give me a call. "Just don't throw anything away!", he warned.

Jacob is a buyer for a large department store with outlets throughout America and Europe. He is out of town seven months a year. Because he is away so often, he accumulates an enormous amount of mail. The US Postal Service attests to the fact that contemporary Americans get more mail in one month than their parents did in an entire year, and more mail in one year than their grandparents received in a lifetime! Jacob's mail is a major source of clutter in his office. Frances is allowed to sort the mail only superficially. Though she knows some of it is junk mail, Jacob prefers to look through all of his mail when he is in his office.

Frances and I buy three large plastic bins that resemble laundry baskets but are slightly smaller and better looking. On the red plastic bin she affixes a handwritten sign that reads "Hot". She and Jacob agree that he must attend to the Hot mail within three days of his return from any trip. The yellow bin Frances entitles "Soon". Jacob pledges to attend to Soon within a week of his return. On the green bin is a sign that reads "Fat Chance". If Jacob does not get to this material within a month, Frances has permission to dump it.

Frances and Jacob have also supplied themselves with lots of red, yellow, and green removable adhesive dots which also mean Hot, Soon, and Fat Chance. All documentation, memorandums, and papers which pass between them must have a colored dot on it indicating its status. (The dots are removable in case the status of the document changes.) Frances even affixes a dot to every phone message she passes along to Jacob. The entire paperflow of the office is color-coded. When Jacob travels, Frances sends him off with a red file folder filled with Hot materials to review on his trip.

Frances tells me a funny story. Jacob is talking with Frances on a pay phone at the airport. Frances is at the office describing a stack of documents, one by one, to Jacob. He, on the other end of the line, responds with the words Red, Yellow, or Green and Frances dutifully dots each document according to Jacob's instruction. Behind Jacob, a long line is growing of people eager to use the pay phone. All they can hear is this grown man repeating Red, Yellow, or Green. Thinking that Jacob might "not be playing with a full deck", a woman waiting to use the pay phone alerts a security guard. The security guard walks up to Jacob and says, "Okay buddy! My uniform is blue and you are going to be in big trouble if you don't get off that phone!"

Color appeals to us both visually and emotionally. Transparent or clear objects perform somewhat differently than color. Containers that are clear enable people to see right through them. Visual organizing tasks such as storing, are obviously enhanced by using transparency.

But there may be another benefit to visual organizing – it may improve executive functioning. When one thinks of executive functioning it may bring to mind being a good executive, someone who can delegate; make important decisions; and determine priorities. But executive functioning actually refers to the ability to execute. The abilities associated with executive functioning are scattered about our neurology, but transparency and color-coding seem to enhance our capacity to execute, an important organizing skill.

Business Is In The Bag

"I can't think when everything is filed away," notes Rupert. "I lose a sense of the big picture when all the little details are stored in file folders and hidden out of sight. I don't see how things fit together, or what comes first, then second, and so forth. When all my work is out and exposed in front of me, chaotic as it may look, I feel more organized."

Rupert's work sure is exposed. It's all on the floor. Rupert uses the floor as his filing system. Neat stacks of paper checkerboard the floor of his home office. The stacks are about three inches from each other side by side in long rows. There is a one-foot-wide alley running down the middle of the office floor for transit between the rows of paper, and about a foot of free space around the perimeter of the office. It reminds me of a well-planned garden.

Long ago Rupert gave up on filing cabinets, except for the most archival of information. "Deep, dark holes," he calls them. He uses his desk only for projects he is engaged in at the moment. But the floor is really his system for staying on top of everything, quite literally.

The floor is the filing system of preference for several of my clients who are architects, artists, and, like Rupert, engineers. It doesn't take a rocket scientist to figure out why. The floor helps such intensely visually-oriented people "see" their papers. And, if it were totally up to him, Rupert might not change a thing, except for the following fact: Rupert stands six feet four inches high. His chiropractic bills are causing him almost as much pain as his back. He simply cannot bend and squat all day every day. And nobody else can help him because they don't understand his unconventional system.

Rupert and I need to find an organizing system that reveals his papers but somehow raises them from the floor. I look around. Blueprints of engineering drawings hang from plan racks. Plan racks are wooden or metal contraptions that work kind of like a clothesline. Instead of clothespins, however, rubber clasps grip the blueprints and hang them from the racks.

"I wonder if we can hang up your documents like blueprints," I say aloud, not even sure what I mean yet.

"Hang up the documents? But how?"

"What about food storage bags?"

Amused, Rupert leads me to his kitchen. In the kitchen, which is upstairs from his office, he has rolls of wax paper, small sandwich bags, aluminum foil, and plastic wrap, but no food storage bags. Rupert remembers the freezer in the basement. There, above the freezer on a shelf, is a good supply of large freezer bags. They even have a strip on them for writing the contents and the date.

I am overjoyed. Rupert is genuinely underwhelmed. I cannot blame him. The idea does seem a little over the edge.

Back at his office, I bend down and scoop up one neat stack of papers from the floor and pitch it into a freezer bag. I seal the top and Rupert writes on the bag "Johnson Specs" and adds a due date. We clip the bag onto the plan rack next to the Johnson blueprints.

We insert all of Rupert's stacked documents inside freezer bags and hang them up like bizarre laundry. "The thing I like about the freezer bags is that my work is revealed to me all at once. Maybe other people would find that overwhelming, but to me, if I can't see it, I don't do it. I need the constant visual cues to prompt me to action."

Rose invented an adaptation of the freezer bag system. She has many small projects in different stages of completion and, as she has gotten older, she has found it more and more difficult to keep track of everything. Like Rupert, unless she can see it, she can't do it. Rose has attached freezer bags to skirt hangers. One project goes in each freezer bag and a big label is affixed to each one. She hangs the skirt hangers on her bathroom and bedroom doors!

People who organize visually have an abundance of tools available to them. Graphs, charts, and erasable calendars help to organize workflow, tasks, and goals. Mountable calendars, schedules, and timelines are unbeatable time management aids. Color-code your filing system and you can instantly tell where any file belongs. Different colored bins, baskets, or containers of all types can be used to visually sort, batch or prioritize just about anything. Transparency, whether clear or colorful, has a dual advantage. It supports visual organizing **and** executive functioning. A list of products that *reveal instead of conceal* follows. One of my favorites is the Big Bag Floor Rack system. It's commonly used in schools and libraries, but you can easily adapt it to your own needs.

36"

Big Bag Floor Rack System by Monaco

Organizing styles reflect our learning style. Identifying your specific learning style can be a helpful exercise and I urge you to visit your library or bookstore for materials on the topic. Relative to chronic disorganization, the precise learning style you have is less important than the recognition that a diversity of learning and organizing styles does exist. Try them all! An auditory organizing method may aid you greatly on the job. Visual products added to your organizing methods at home might make tremendous breakthroughs. And who knows what potential kinesthetic organizing might have for time management or other areas of organizing. You are already an unconventional organizer. You might as well go all the way!

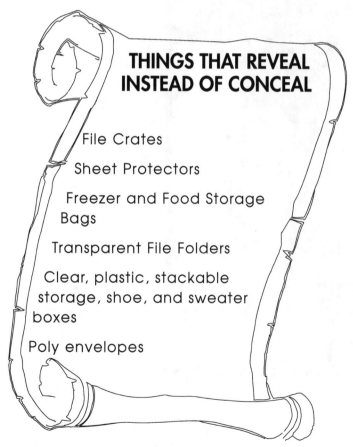

THINGS THAT REVEAL INSTEAD OF CONCEAL

File Crates

Sheet Protectors

Freezer and Food Storage Bags

Transparent File Folders

Clear, plastic, stackable storage, shoe, and sweater boxes

Poly envelopes

CHAPTER 4

WHOLISTIC ORGANIZING

Wholistic organizing refers to the process of using organizing methods that seek to build-up rather than to breakdown. Wholistic organizing runs counter-intuitive to conventional organizing. Breaking things down is the bedrock of most conventional organizing methods. Think about it. When your home needs organizing, it makes sense to break it down into manageable pieces rather than attempt to tackle the whole house. You begin with a single room. If a single room is daunting; a single closet, or even one closet shelf might be the most practical place to start. A disorganized office might best be approached by organizing the desk or even a single drawer of the desk first. Even time management is broken down. Missions are distilled down into goals which are broken down into objectives. Objectives are further broken down into monthly and weekly schedules which are finally expressed as daily to-dos. Even if you wanted to organize your entire house or office all at once, you could not do it.

As a practical matter, we often have no choice but to begin with a part rather than a whole. The problem is, chronically disorganized people tend to find the process of breaking things down, of making parts out of a whole, a fragmenting experience. However overwhelming the whole may be, it is still an unfragmented (albeit disorganized) big picture which chronically disorganized people find comforting.

This feeling of fragmentation, of losing the big picture, is a major organizing obstacle. We are left with a dilemma. On the one hand, practically speaking, we need to break down large, complex, and overwhelming organizing projects into small, manageable pieces. On the other hand, conventional organizing, with its insistence on breaking things down, obliterates the big picture and promotes fragmentation.

This dilemma is resolved with themes and imagery – wholistic organizing methods which retain a sense of the whole even while it is being broken down and transformed.

Anatomy of an Office

Pete is one of those lucky middle managers who has survived round after round of downsizing, rightsizing, and re-engineering. Each year his location on the company's organizational chart moves but he manages to hold onto his job. Pete called me after the latest round of layoffs.

"My job is so stressful. I've got to keep my feet planted on the ground, get my hands on things, and keep my eye on the ball," Pete says. I make a mental note of his many allusions to the human body and we set up a time to get together.

Pete meets me in the lobby of his building. We sit down on a couple of leather chairs and he talks about why he saves paper and how disorganized his office is. Then we enter the elevator and Pete continues talking, offering me more background information about his disorganization. When we exit the elevator I think we will finally go into his office. Instead he takes me to the conference room. Seated once more, Pete continues to explain his clutter habits.

Finally we walk down the corridor to his office. The office door is closed. Pete does not open it. Instead he stretches out his arms in front of him and begins to do a kind of push-up on the wall, all the while continuing to talk.

Now, I can talk with the best of them. I love to talk. But, to me, talking, background information, and self-analysis are not nearly as informative as actually *seeing* what Pete is contending with. He is having the hardest time just opening the door to show me his office. His talking is basically a stall.

"Two things you should know about me, Pete. One is that I have no sense of appall, and the other is that I will not judge you as a person by the way your office looks."

"I appreciate your telling me these things. The truth is, I can't even look at my office anymore. When I open this door it's like being hit by a wave."

"I understand. I think I have something here that might help. Try this."

From inside my rather large pocketbook I take out my secret weapon: a cardboard paper towel tube. The tube is covered with tiger-striped fabric. "I am going to open the door. When I do, you look through the tube and tell me what you see," I instruct Pete.

I open the door slowly and, when it is wide open, he lifts the tube to his eye and takes a look inside. "I see my credenza."

"Good, now slowly move the tube an inch to the left and stop and tell me what you see."

"I see my desk."

The tube enables Pete to narrow his visual field. An expert in learning disabilities taught me that visual field means what a person sees at any given time. If you put two people in a furnished room, one will see the couch first, then a chair next, then maybe a lamp, and finally, a picture on the wall. But the other person might see everything in the room – the couch, the chairs, the lamps and the pictures, all at once. This latter phenomenon is called a wide visual field. People with a wide visual field can feel overwhelmed easily.

"Your office feels like a big wave crashing in on you because you see it all at once. The cardboard tube helps you see it in smaller parts which we can organize one at a time." Feeling less overwhelmed, Pete finally steps inside his office and I follow closing the door behind us hoping he won't lose his nerve and walk out.

"Now scan the interior of the office and choose a spot where you would like to begin." With the tube still at his eye, like a pirate with a spyglass, he says, "That mess on the window sill. I definitely would like to start there."

The window sill seems like a good place to start. When we unclutter it, Pete will feel a real sense of accomplishment. At least, this is what I think, but it turns out that I am wrong.

Pete is a very deliberate, slow sorter, which no doubt contributes to his chronicness. He studies each piece of paper carefully. Often he inefficiently walks single pieces of paper over to different locations in the office. After what seems like a painfully long time, the window sill is finally cleared of clutter. But rather than a sense of accomplishment, he feels frustrated. "At this rate, we'll need a year to organize this office."

I need to find a way for Pete to feel *in control of his entire office* more quickly. The anatomy references he used earlier to describe his office pop into my mind. "When you first called me on the phone, you said you had to 'get your feet on the ground, your hands on things, and your eye on the ball.' Do you remember?"

"Yes, but I don't think I follow your point."

"My point is why don't we organize your office with the theme of a human body!"

"You know, Judith, if it was not for your reputation for helping chronically disorganized people like me, I would say you are a little strange."

"Well, maybe being a little strange is what it takes to make a breakthrough. Let me explain. I think we can organize your office based on body parts. Where do you think the brain of your office is?"

"Got to be the computer area. It's where I do Internet research and think through the information I gather. It's definitely the brains of the office."

"Let's put your documents related to thinking and research near the brain (the computer). Does your office have a stomach?"

"It certainly does. I sit on that couch over there with my feet up on the coffee table and I digest tons of reports." We move all of Pete's reports over to the Stomach.

To aid us in our reorganization of Pete's office on the basis of anatomy, I make a rough drawing of a human body, which appears below. We hang an athletic bag on the doorknob. This is Pete's Legs. In the athletic bag are errands he must run (film to develop, magazines to take home, pictures to frame, etc.). Pete's Mouth is the phone and fax. Beside it we put calls to return, calls to initiate, and any documents related to those calls.

"This stuff stinks!" Pete exclaims, holding a personnel evaluation form in his hand. "I hate filling out evaluations." We put stinky documents in a three-ring binder called the Nose and shelve it on the bookcase.

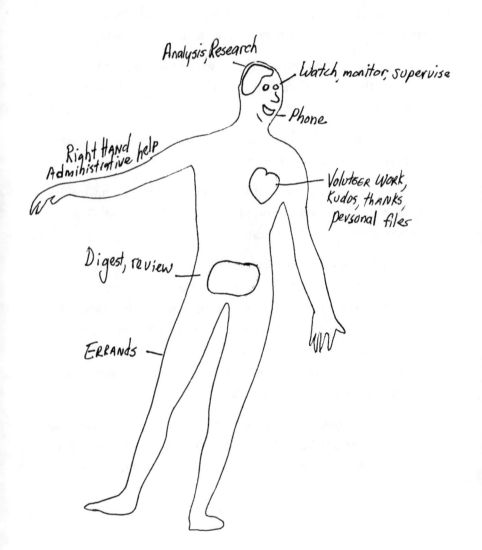

Pete and I break his office down into different areas, but because all the areas are associated with a single theme, in this case the human body, his office does not feel fragmented. To Pete, the office continues to exist as a whole even though it has parts. It is this concept of the whole, the theme, that makes it possible for him to organize his office without feeling overwhelmed by its fragments.

I visit Pete a few months after "the operation" we performed on his office. On his credenza he has arranged a set of files to hold papers related to his volunteer work at the children's shelter and the Boys & Girls Club. He calls the credenza his Heart.

Draft Your Administrative Assistant to Help You!

Pete is chronically disorganized and has great difficulty maintaining organization. It is essential that his administrative assistant, Lois, learn how to use the human body theme to keep him organized.

Pete and I involve Lois in sorting and organizing the documentation in his office, and in rearranging furniture. It takes ten hours over the course of two weeks, but because Lois has been involved in the organizing-by-theme process from the beginning, she can administratively support Pete.

Lois tells a funny story of a client waiting to see Pete. The client is seated in the waiting area, reading a magazine. Lois sits opposite the client at her reception desk. Pete walks into the waiting area and hands Lois a document. "Please chew this," he says to her. Lois and Pete laugh out loud at the client's shocked expression. "Chew" is their anatomical reference to the paper shredder!

SPACE TRAVEL

Janet's office is organized around a travel theme. She is a very successful cellular phone saleswoman in an extremely competitive field, and is on the road constantly. Like many women, Janet is very attuned to landmarks. A map may help her arrive at a destination, but landmarks supply her directional needs. Janet can navigate a strange city immediately without getting lost by recalling landmarks – like that her hotel is right off the exit with the WalMart shopping center, or that the restaurant where she is meeting a customer tomorrow is directly across the street from Burger King.

Landmarks are a natural tool to use for organizing Janet's office. Paperweights make excellent office landmarks. They indicate exactly where certain items are. A heavy quartz owl paperweight sits atop clippings from magazines and articles downloaded from the World Wide Web. "If I am as wise as an owl, maybe I'll be more successful," Janet reasons. The Rotary Club awarded Janet a bronze lion paperweight. The lion is king of the jungle. Janet keeps memos from her boss under the lion.

The most interesting aspect of Janet's travel theme is her traffic signs. She thought, with all the driving she does, perhaps traffic signs might help her be as organized in her office as she is on the road. I bought the signs in a specialized store that sells educational toys and pedagogical games for teachers and parents.

A stop sign mounted on the wall directly over Janet's small conference table is a kind of "the buck stops here" symbol to Janet. It is where customer complaints and issues requiring her prompt, personal attention land. A yield sign hangs on the wall above her credenza. "Yielding" is to Janet what time management experts call delegating. The yield sign reminds her to delegate or yield work over to others. Under it are the materials for Janet's secretary.

The use of a travel theme organizes Janet. Travel is a world of symbols and objects she relates to easily. The travel theme imposes a kind of wholistic order on the chaos of Janet's office. But because she is chronically disorganized, keeping up her office is still a challenge.

Use Checklists!

Janet benefits from "Departure" and "Arrival" checklists. Checklists of all kinds are excellent anti-chronic devices. A checklist developed in preparation for and after a trip; a complex project; or a busy season is a great asset to a chronically disorganized person. Janet and her secretary meet to develop a Departure checklist one week before Janet leaves. It details standard tasks, like packing adequate promotional literature and making sure Janet has her car phone plugged in. The list also details variable tasks including calls her secretary must make in Janet's absence. The Arrival checklist includes turning in expense reports, sending out thank-you notes, and other follow-up tasks that always accompany a sales trip.

Go shopping!

Another effective organizing theme is that of a store. Denslow Brown, a professional organizer, has organized a client's workshop and garage on the model of a hardware store. Using an elaborate set of bins, pegboards, shelves, and containers, the client "shops" in his own workshop for what he needs. His job is to keep the workshop and garage properly stocked "for the next customer." He must return all the tools and supplies to their right places when he is finished using them.

Another colleague of mine takes the store theme one step further. She actually has her client shop in her own home! Several times a year, she and her client walk through the house with a shopping list. They "shop" for the items on the list. This process reacquaints the client with what she already owns, reminds her of where items are kept, and eliminates excess shopping and redundant purchases. "I thought I needed to buy a tablecloth. But after "shopping" I discovered I already own two of them," the client said.

CLINGING TO THE FUTURE

People keep things for many, many reasons. Much excessive saving revolves around the past – mementos of earlier phases of our life; souvenirs from vacations taken long ago; keepsakes from hundreds of occasions; awards and trophies honoring past achievements; and clothing to remind us of a size we no longer are. The most comprehensive book I have ever read on saving is called *Clutter's Last Stand*, by Don Aslett. Aslett says:

> Should we choose to spend our lives collecting, preserving, and storing artifacts and inactive possessions we will find ourselves...wandering past the precious moment of life at hand...our past things have value, but the secret is to not let charm turn into chains, sentiment become a sentence...only you know the moment when collectibles have become clutter in your life...

The "moment" when collectibles turn into clutter is not always apparent. Some chronically disorganized people miss it altogether.

But an organizing theme I call Clinging To The Future can help. Kevin and I used it to organize his home.

Kevin's home is filled to the rafters with stuff of all kinds. This stuff is so vast and jumbled it is impossible to tell what is junk and what is not. Kevin has tried to break it down. "In an effort to clear off the couch, I clutter up the floor so much I can hardly walk around. Then I try to clear up the floor and end up just cluttering the couch again. It feels like 'switching dishes'." Switching dishes is a Southern expression for moving things from one place to another but not really changing anything.

Kevin and I designate an extra bedroom of the house as the Past. We gather up from the couch, floor, dining room table, and all the other parts of the house everything that draws its meaning from the past, or preserves the past. The Past contains trophies, paid bills, tax records, boxes of photographs and scrapbooks, clothes that do not fit, items inherited from other family members but that Kevin no longer wants, old magazines and used greeting cards. All of these things go in the extra bedroom, the Past.

We designate the den as the Present. The Present holds current magazines, bills due for payment, recent photographs awaiting framing, warranties for appliances Kevin still owns, clothes that fit, money (yes, we found six dollars' worth of loose change and a wallet with seventeen dollars in it!), and all the things throughout the house relevant to the present. We stow all these things in the den.

Kevin's home office is the Future. The Future stores newspaper clippings of investment ideas, vacation brochures, flyers and invitations about upcoming events, new flowerpots Kevin won't need to use until the Spring, recent computer catalogues (Kevin is researching a computer to replace his old one), blank video tapes, unread books, and unused greeting cards.

The extra bedroom completely fills up with the Past. This is a very helpful development. Kevin can now sensuously see how much space the Past takes up in his home. It helps him realize how much the Past takes up in his life. This realization is just the motivation Kevin needs to deal with the Past. We recycle the magazines older than one year, mount the trophies on the mantel in the den, box up the tax records and move them to the attic, throw away used greeting cards, and find a nice spot for photographs and scrapbooks on the bookcase. Now that the extra bedroom has been liberated from the Past, it can begin to be used as a guest bedroom.

Once the Past is organized, we begin to work on the Future. Kevin and I take out his planner and actually schedule a time for him to review his future investment ideas. It's a natural year-end activity, but unless scheduled, it will never happen. Now he can file this material away in his filing cabinet because the appointment, and not the materials themselves, will remind Kevin of his task.

Kevin's vacation time is the second week of August. To make sure he has adequate time to look over his vacation brochures, and purchase the best airline tickets, we schedule a "Plan Vacation" appointment four weeks ahead. Now that he has a calendar entry to remind him to plan his vacation, Kevin can file the vacation brochures away. Kevin tosses away the flyers and invitations piled on his desk. Instead he decides which he wants to attend, and notes the dates on his calendar.

We make a calendar entry in February for Kevin to begin his re-potting and other Spring gardening chores, and we move the flower pots out of the office to his backyard shed. The blank video tapes and unused greeting cards remain in the Future (a.k.a. the home office) so Kevin will know exactly where they are when he needs them. Books for leisure reading are placed on the nightstand next to his bed. With a little planning and time management, the Future is more organized.

The den, where the Present resides, is not quite full, but it is easy for Kevin to see that if he neglects to attend to the Present, it will overflow his den. The catalogues Kevin is using to research a new computer, graduate from the Future to the Present so that he will deal with it sooner. We disperse current magazines to all the places in the house where Kevin reads. (A few remain in a basket by the couch in the den. Several are put in the bathroom. And a few go by Kevin's bed.) The photographs for framing are put in the car, a constant reminder to Kevin to stop at the frame store. Kevin pays his bills in the den, so we set up a mini bill paying center there, complete with stamps, envelopes, and last month's bills.

The timeline theme is a breakthrough for Kevin. It enables him to breakdown the organizing of his home into manageable parts but grounds him with a theme at the same time. Now when clutter accumulates in Kevin's home, he goes through it with the Past, Present, or Future in mind. If it's relevant to the Present, it goes right to the den for action. If it regards the Future, the task is scheduled, then the object itself is put away where it belongs. And if it's regarding the Past, Kevin scrutinizes it first to decide if he needs it at all. He no longer tolerates the Past taking over his home.

IMAGERY

We all have a "mind's eye," a way of creating images mentally in our minds. This process is called imagery. Imagery is a useful organizing method. Imagery turns seemingly abstract organizing problems into mental pictures. Then the mental pictures can be converted into concrete solutions.

We used imagery for organizing Fran who has the worst case of "Rolodex™ eruptus" I have ever seen. Business cards are scattered like leaves all over her office. Like a magician's card trick they appear in every pocket of her clothes. Her briefcase and pocketbook burst with them. Business cards, Rolodex™ cards, napkins with names and phone numbers, and tiny slips of paper with names and addresses stock every drawer, nook, and cranny.

Fran is an insurance agent. She sells more insurance in the South than anyone else because she ensures that anyone who needs anything, not just insurance, is able to hook up with someone who provides it. She is a master networker. Fran does not really collect business cards, she collects people.

I have Fran close her eyes and conjure up an image of a real person for each business card, napkin, or note she owns. She imagines that person actually standing in the room with us. This imagery makes it easy for Fran to decide whether that person should stay or be asked to leave (e.g., should the business card be kept or tossed).

Fran imagines all these people at a cocktail party in her home. They are holding hors d'oeuvres and getting along nicely with each other, and saying nice things about her. Others, however, are vague, faceless people Fran can hardly remember. And several seem arrogant or rude when brought to life. Fran discards the business cards of these latter two groups.

Fran also uses a kind of Greenwich Village imagery. She fills the room with artists, actors, writers, and an occasional palm reader, all representations of actual business cards. In the full-blown images of real people, Fran finds some of these people to be interesting. Others are past relations that have little meaning to her now, and so she discards them.

A large crowd of people in the room are wearing suits: lawyers, accountants, financial planners, insurance agents, and realtors. "There are way too many suits in this room," Fran complains, and she asks those that don't seem familiar to her to leave. Their business cards are tossed away.

The imagery of each business card being an actual person occupying her house is powerful for Fran. It enables her to make decisions about keeping or tossing the cards. In her words, imagery "changes my business card mess from an unruly mob into a real network of people."

Much Ado About Something

Imagery as an organizing method is a natural for artists and creative people like Julius.

Julius is an under-employed actor who runs the telemarketing operation of one of Atlanta's largest performing arts organizations. He is extremely good at it. His "boiler room" is light and airy with not a hint of cigarette smoke. His telemarketers, mostly artists and musicians waiting for their big break, make hundreds of calls with the special flourish of enthusiasm only performers can summon. Julius inspires his telemarketers with short readings from Shakespeare, scenes from contemporary plays, and poetry readings. In addition to their base salary and bonuses; high-producing telemarketers win voice lessons, art supplies, and free tickets to cultural events. At the end of the evening, the telemarketer with the most fund-raising success is lifted high into the air atop the shoulders of her compatriots and led by Julius himself on a celebratory parade around the room, complete with song, dance, and general mayhem. In short, the whole operation makes a point of making a scene.

Julius is great at rallying his troops to reach fund-raising goals. His organizing skills, on the other hand, are lacking. He is chronically disorganized. His particular downfall is gathering materials for reports, compiling reports, and presenting these reports to the Board of Directors. Julius can never find the materials he needs for the reports. The tedium of preparing reports overwhelms him, and his presentations to the Board are ill-prepared. Unless he improves pronto, Julius will lose his job. I am told this by his immediate supervisor, Kate, who adores him but is under pressure from the Board of Directors, and wants to know if I can save Julius' job.

There is a theory within the business community – and shared by the artistic community – that creative types are incapable of being well-organized. I think the theory goes something like this – an artist is a creative person; creativity/art is the direct opposite of business/organization; therefore, one can hardly expect an artist to be organized.

Largely, this is a stereotype. I've met many actors and artists who are organizing experts – juggling multiple jobs, rehearsals, showings, lessons and all manner of obligations. But, like most stereotypes, this one has a grain of truth. The challenge is to discover ways of bringing imagery and other artistic strengths of creative people into the organizing process.

"Yes, I can help Julius," I answer Kate, "but certainly not under the pressure of saving Julius' job. Only Julius can do that," I remind her.

I encourage Julius to "make a scene" whenever he performs an organizing act. For instance, he has a file called "Week-End Tally". He calls one of his telemarketers into the filing room. While he files the folder, the telemarketer "witnesses" the act. In a mock court-like procedure, he has her hold up her right hand and put her left on a zip code book. She swears that Julius has filed the folder under Week-End Tally. Then Julius dismisses his witness/telemarketer.

This somewhat elaborate little play enables Julius to fix an image in his mind of the file folder and its placement in the file. Sometimes he pretends he has a camera in his hand and he takes a mock photograph of the file.

In his book *ADD Success Stories*, Thom Hartmann collects stories from individuals who have Attention Deficit Disorder. One story called "Original Awareness" tells of a man who is always forgetting his wallet or where he has parked his car, particularly when he is running late and already distracted and nervous:

> When I'm late at the airport, I'll make a point of visually imprinting my parking location. I'll put my eyes on the section signs for a full minute, even if I'm running.

Essentially, this gentleman uses imagery to remind him of his parking spot. Such techniques may seem odd or anti-logical, but they work well for people who are chronically disorganized.

To cope with the tedium of preparing reports, Julius draws on the imagery of Ebenezer Scrooge in Dickens' classic novel, *A Christmas Carol*. He puts on a somewhat ratty sweater and sits hunched over at his desk. He has attached a feather to his pen with a rubber band. In the winter he turns down the heat, and in the summer he turns off the air conditioner. He makes himself a little uncomfortable and proceeds to compile the reports. To end his misery, he works quickly and does not agonize over them as before.

"Ladies and gentlemen, I give you the fund-raising report!" Julius exclaims flamboyantly, as his assistant distributes bound reports to the Board members, who are now accustomed to Julius' bold entrances. Instead of simply sitting at his place at the conference table reciting information, Julius now uses colorful flip chart pages to make his point about fund-raising progress. Sometimes he even wears a cape or a magician's hat!

Imagery, like themes, can be drawn from a person's occupation, passions, strengths, and even fears! I once worked with Nancy, a writer. She loved to write magazine articles, but deadlines terrified her. When she did make a deadline, it was always an intensely stressful experience. On occasion, she missed a deadline completely. We created an image of a little monster called Deadline. He is a short, ugly thing with a ferocious appetite. To be appeased, Deadline needs to be fed (writing) daily. As long as Nancy feeds Deadline daily, she meets her deadlines.

THEMES AND IMAGERY IDEAS

The Human Body

Travel, Space Travel

Stores, Shopping

Timeline

Scenes from a Play or a Novel

War Room, Command Central

A Factory

Sports

Board Games

CHAPTER 5

SOCIAL ORGANIZING

Conquering chronic disorganization requires innovative organizing approaches that embrace emotions; are sensitive to learning/organizing style differences; and are wholistic. However, we are all unique individuals so not every approach, method, or technique for conquering chronic disorganization will work for every person. But there is one necessity for conquering chronic disorganization that no chronically disorganized person can do without. It speaks to the very heart of the chronicness of chronic disorganization. I call it social organizing.

In order to maintain organizing success, a chronically disorganized person must involve other people in the process. Social organizing is the term used to describe the ongoing use of other people in the organizing process. Perhaps you have noticed that most of the anti-chronic devices discussed so far involve other people. That is because the chronicness of chronic disorganization cannot be overcome alone. It is not unlike learning to speak in front of other people. Public speaking, though it may be practiced in private, cannot be mastered without actually speaking in public. If you are chronically disorganized, organizing must become a social, rather than an individual, activity.

One reason for the necessity of organizing socially has simply to do with morale. All chronically disorganized people find getting organized to be overwhelming. Without "troops," even if it is only one other person, that sense of being overwhelmed makes organizing too daunting and frustrating. Once this happens, the effort to organize ceases. Then organizing looms even larger, which makes it even more overwhelming, and the downward cycle continues. Social organizing breaks this cycle. Morale remains high and overwhelm remains low, so organizing can proceed.

Another reason organizing must be social and not solitary is that a chronically disorganized person needs a body double. A body double provides you with an anchor and a mirror. With a body double, your new-found level of organization can be maintained. Body doubling is described in greater detail below.

Social organizing might be a difficult concept to grasp. After all, when Mom said, "Clean up your room," she never meant anything other than you doing it by yourself. In American culture, whenever we speak of success, or overcoming something, we almost always associate it with individual action. Indeed, to be totally self-reliant has become a mark of success. But to really conquer chronic disorganization, to keep disorganization from returning to undermine your quality of life, you must organize socially. Working alone is a prescription for disaster.

This does not mean that there are not things you must do as an individual. There most certainly are steps you, and you alone, must take to get and stay organized. The most important among these is to determine just how you will involve other people in your organizing efforts.

THE BODY DOUBLE

When I walk into Zita's home I am very surprised. Conditioned to see clutter, I am taken aback that all the sofas and chairs are, in fact, clear of clutter. The dining room table is set with beautiful placemats, silverware, and a floral centerpiece. The credenza displays antique-framed photographs and is adorned with silver candlesticks. There are no unopened stacks of mail and no back issues of magazines or catalogues. I can only surmise that Zita and I have yet to enter "the secret room."

The secret room is that area of one's house that hides a reposi-tory of unbridled clutter behind a closed door. As Zita continues to conduct our tour through her grand, neat home, I am certain the secret room must lie just down the hall. Instead, we enter a beauti-fully appointed study with Persian rugs, Grecian urns, and fine furni-ture. The desk, an antique rolltop with many exquisite, handcarved cubbies, contains what appear to be bills, mail, and the like. I will concede that these little cubbies are stuffed, but the usual evidence of chronic disorganization seems lacking. So I am a little mystified by Zita's need for help.

"Here is my problem," Zita says, motioning for me to sit down beside her at the desk. I sit, waiting for her to reveal to me her orga-nizing problem and think perhaps she has lost her train of thought, but she explains nothing. Instead, Zita methodically sorts through a cubby. In silence, she slices an envelope open with a handsome letter opener, reads the contents to herself, and tosses it into an ornately decorated waste basket. She slices another envelope open, and determining it is an unpaid bill, quietly opens her checkbook which is handily tucked inside another cubby. Zita writes the check and hands it to me together with the return envelope. I stuff the check inside and seal the envelope while she sorts through another cubby.

We work silently as Zita continues to open envelopes, pay bills, or toss garbage away. Occasionally she comments about an overdue bill or remarks about the wastefulness of perfectly good trees. I respond with a word or two, but mainly she sticks to her slicing, I stick to putting checks in envelopes, and we work at a quiet tempo.

As I work with Zita, my mind begins to wander. I begin to imagine myself at a quilting bee with the soft din of needles and thread and small talk (small, not in the sense of trivial, but in the economy-of-words, understated sense). I am lost in this image when, precisely one hour after we begin, Zita puts her letter opener down and rises from her chair.

"Well, my dear, that was very helpful. You are a good organizer. Here is your check and I shall call you again soon."

"Thank you," I respond, a little stunned, walking with her to the front door. "Do you mind if I ask you a question?"

"Certainly, dear."

"What was it about our time together that you found so helpful?"

"Why your presence, dear. Not that I am a lonely old woman. Lord, no. My family visits often, and I have wonderful friends and a lot of things to occupy my time. But I simply cannot go through my mail or my papers alone. I must have you near in order to do it. Have a nice day, dear."

According to Linda Anderson, a colleague of mine and a coach for adults with ADD, I am Zita's body double. A body double functions as an anchor. The presence of a human anchor focuses another person and makes it possible for her to ignore distractions. My body doubling seems like not much more than occupying space, yet it creates an anchor for Zita. Her mind translates the body double experience as, "I cannot leave this place until I am finished, and neither can my body double!" She is anchored to her organizing tasks by this responsibility.

Anderson says that the second positive effect of body doubling is that of a mirror. As I sit by Zita's side, barely involved, I reflect back to her a model of what concentrated organizing looks like. This reflection says: "This is me; I am focused; I am doing organizing now and nothing else."

I used to believe that only a professional organizer could body double because they are practiced at being passive yet supportive; encouraging but not judgmental; and they tend to be more patient than family members or friends. But Jack, Beth's husband, taught me that other people can be excellent body doubles! Jack is well-organized and Beth is chronically disorganized. They have been married for a long time but "the organizing wars" have always been a sore spot. Though Beth appreciates Jack's organizing skills, she has not been able to model them. Jack, though sensitive to Beth's organizing challenges, grows impatient with her. I suggest that instead of actively attempting to organize Beth, Jack should body double for her. In this new passive role, Jack putters with his own work while Beth organizes her desk. They work side-by-side in this fashion for hours. Everyone is satisfied and the "wars" are now reduced to occasional polite skirmishes.

RULES FOR YOUR BODY DOUBLE

A body double is not an active assistant.

A body double's principal job is to occupy space while you do organizing chores.

A body double must be quiet and non-distracting.

A body double should perform small, unobtrusive tasks while you organize. Opening the mail, labeling file folders, folding clothes, or packing books in cartons, are good body double tasks.

A body double cannot be judgemental.

A body double must be patient and able to sit still for long periods of time.

THE CREW

Another effective social organizing technique is the crew. Lester has three generations of clutter in his home. His adult children are the end of his family line. Lester is committed to passing on to his children only the best possessions of their family tree "without all the weeds and brambles. My children could spend the rest of their lives just going through all the cartons and clutter if I don't do something about it now," Lester tells me as we stand at the top of the basement stairs peering down at cartons, furniture, books, and other clutter that fills the entire basement.

"I'll undertake this project if you let me bring in a crew," I say. "Otherwise, it will take the greater part of a year to accomplish. In that time, you might become disheartened and I might throw my back out!"

A crew consists of a supervisor, at least one assistant, and the chronically disorganized person who is called the owner (he owns the clutter). I explain that the job of the crew is to presort all the clutter so the owner can reduce its quantity. A presort organizes the clutter broadly by agreed-upon categories. Earlier in this book, we said that categories are sometimes not a good organizing tool for chronically disorganized people. But broad categorization does work under presort conditions because the clutter is dormant. Dormant clutter is clutter that is simply being warehoused. The owner's sole motivation for organizing the clutter is to physically reduce the quantity of clutter being warehoused. If something emerges from a presort that is useable, pleasurable, or saleable, all the better, but that is not the main goal.

Once these presort categories are in place the crew is deliberately designed to function without the constant presence of the owner. "Frankly, I'm relieved," Lester remarks. "My chronic disorganization will just hold you back." Actually chronic disorganization will hold Lester back. Lester's habitual tendency to keep things will always overpower his judgement. The crew and the presort will give him the opportunity to use his judgement.

Lester and I agree on the presort categories, which include: Photographs, Housewares, Books, Stationery Supplies, Artwork/Framed Pictures, Magazines, Furniture and Appliances.

My assistant, trained in large-scale presorts, writes these categories on neon paper signs in big block letters and posts the signs along the basement walls. The crew then sorts all the materials in the basement under the appropriate signs. The few errors we no doubt make in categorizing this vast quantity of material, are far outweighed by the cost in time and expense that absolute precision would require.

The job rapidly takes on the appearance of a well-organized warehouse. As we proceed with the presort, other categories emerge. It seems most of the men and a good deal of the women in Lester's genealogy served in the armed forces. Medals, weapons, uniforms, and military memorabilia are plentiful, and so we add a category called Military.

One entire wall of the basement is devoted to Recommended Refuse. This is key to a presort. It is here that our crew is authorized to stack broken furniture, empty boxes, soiled documents and books, damaged artwork, and anything insect-infested. The crew takes no liberties in discarding anything. Instead we take advantage of the Recommended Refuse category. As owner, one of Lester's assignments is to check in on the presorting every two days. When he visits, he does a "sampling" of the Recommended Refuse pile. He closes his eyes and randomly selects ten items from the

Recommended Refuse stack. If eight of the ten items are indeed refuse, the entire pile is arranged for disposal. (The crew has never scored less than 80%). Lester has to make the executive decisions about whether the refuse is disposed of, recycled, donated or a combination.

During a presort, papers are sorted into five generic types: Financial Papers, whose meanings derive more from numerical data than from words (receipts, bank statements, etc.); Tax documents; Correspondence (hand-written letters and cards); Important Papers (marriage/ birth/ death certificates, legal documents, wills, and deeds); and Loose Papers (a generic term for everything else).

Loose papers are an unknown quantity, especially if they are inherited. We treat them with a sampling method similar to that used in Recommended Refuse. Lester samples twenty loose papers, chosen completely at random. If ten or more of the twenty prove to be worthless, the next foot of loose paper is scooped up and disposed of. He then samples twenty more papers. If ten or more are worthless, another foot of loose paper is disposed of, and so forth. In this way, Lester is able to dispose of loose papers without the tedius chore of examining each one.

How to Assemble a Crew

The Owner

You are the owner of the clutter and a very important part of the crew. Your goal is to reduce the quantity of your clutter quickly. For this you will need to hire a crew supervisor, who will then hire the assistants. I strongly recommend that you interview area professional organizers for the job of supervisor. A professional organizer is often familiar with presort techniques. As a second choice, select a take-charge type person who is well-organized, hard-working and able to supervise others.

You might already know someone like this at your job. Or take a look around your neighborhood. Maybe that young college student at church who organizes the annual charity book sale is available. Or that woman who runs the neighborhood flea market. Once you have found a supervisor, authorize the supervisor to find an assistant(s).

Your next responsibility is to meet with the supervisor to determine key presort categories. You will also be needed to regularly check in on the progress of the presort and make critical on-the-spot decisions. You might be tempted to supervise the presort yourself. This is not a good idea. Let the supervisor do her job but be available to confer regularly.

The Supervisor

The supervisor must be willing to study the presort techniques in this book. It is also the supervisor's job to find, supervise, and ensure the safety of assistants. The assistants should be strong, willing to get their hands a little dirty, able to take direction, and smart enough to bring to the attention of the supervisor any concerns about the value or importance of the clutter. The supervisor works with the owner to identify the most useful presort categories. It is also the supervisor's job to provide the owner with regular status reports, and work with the owner to make disposition decisions.

The Assistant(s)

Family members, mature high school students, friends of the owner, and people with disabilities make excellent assistants, as long as they can work under the leadership of the supervisor. Sometimes a professional organizer will have assistants of her own. An assistant's main job is to understand the presort categories and presort all the clutter. An assistant should also be aware of items of value and bring that to the attention of the supervisor who will discuss it with the owner. Assistants need to work quickly but with safety in mind and must be cooperative with the other assistants.

"I love having the crew here," Lester exclaims. "It kind of feels like a factory atmosphere where things are being produced rather than a graveyard where things are dead. I'm sort of the factory owner; you know, the guy with the nice clean white shirt and tie who dons a hardhat to inspect the situation. I'm involved, but things clearly get done without me."

General Presort Procedures are summarized below. Use the social organizing technique of a crew especially when circumstances create a very large quantity of dormant clutter. These circumstances include absorbing inheritances, melding households with someone else and moving. It is not possible to provide even general guidelines for every category of presort clutter that might arise. Every presort is different, but they are all motivated by one goal: reduction of dormant clutter.

General Presort Procedures

Step 1. Assemble a crew (see previous instructions).

Step 2. Establish generic presort categories for non-paper clutter. Common presort categories include housewares/small appliances, books, stationery supplies, magazines, furniture/furnishings, photographs, artwork, hardware/tools, film/videos/slides/cameras, clothing, and health and beauty items.

Step 3. Establish generic paper categories. These include financial papers (examples include receipts, charge card carbons, bank statements, cancelled checks, investment statements); personal correspondence and greeting cards; tax documents; important papers (marriage/ birth/ death certificates, legal papers, wills, and deeds), and loose papers (pretty much everything else that can't be immediately identified).

Step 4. Devote an area to Recommended Refuse. This is where the crew is authorized to stack broken furniture, empty boxes, soiled clothing, damaged appliances, expired insurance policies, rusted tools, and anything that is insect infested. (Exceptions include damaged photographs, artwork, and personal correspondence.) It is the owner's responsibility to review the Recommended Refuse by using a sampling method.

Step 5. Post brightly colored paper signs along the walls of the presort area, with a different category printed on each in large block letters. The crew will then presort all the clutter under the appropriate signs.

Step 6. Separate housewares/small appliances and stationery supplies into two generic subcategories – "The Best" and "Other". Use The Best yourself. Give away anything you do not want from this category to people you know or arrange to donate it to a worthy cause. Other should always be donated or recycled.

Step 7.   Books are not sorted in any way during a presort because it is too time-consuming. Instead, all books (unless they are damaged) are displayed standing upright with the spine showing, library-style. Arrange the books this way on available bookcases, shelves, mantels, tables, or other surfaces. Later, someone can go through the books spine-by-spine and make decisions about their disposition.

Step 8.   Magazines are treated in the following manner: The oldest twelve magazines and the newest twelve magazines are extracted from the entire collection. If the oldest magazines have any historical value, they are kept, and all the others through the date of the newest twelve are recycled. If the newest magazines have any content value, they are kept, but any older magazines are recycled. If the oldest magazines and the newest magazines all prove to be neither historical nor collectible nor of any value for their content, all the magazines are recycled.

Step 9.   Furniture/furnishings should be arranged as if in a real room. For example, chairs should be arranged around tables, sofas and upholstered chairs should be arranged with end tables and lamps, bookcases should be filled with books, etc. The owner decides what to keep and use, sell, give away to friends and family, or donate. All furniture/furnishings are tagged with these decisions. Furniture that might be antique can be appraised.

Step 10.   Photographs and personal correspondence (hand-written letters, postcards, telegrams, and greeting cards) cannot be discarded during a presort, nor can the time be taken to read and study each. They can be passed along to a family member who is interested in genealogy and can advise you as to which are worth keeping. (Note: this person should mark the identity of the people in the photo and the approximate date of the photo lightly in pencil on the reverse side.) Another method is to display all of the photographs and personal correspondence at the next large family gathering, and let your relatives choose any that they desire.

Step 11.   Artwork should be displayed gallery-style on the walls. The owner can select a limited amount (five or ten pieces) to keep; or give the artwork to friends, family, or charity. If you suspect any are of value, invite an appraiser or an art dealer to view them.

Step 12.   Financial papers and tax documents are sorted by decade, bundled with rubber bands, labeled and stored in marked boxes. Family members might decide later to examine these papers. Or they may decide, with the aid of the decade labels, that some are just too old to be of any use and can be disposed of. Or nothing at all may ever be done with them and they may outlive the humans who created them. For the purposes of a presort, it does not matter.

Step 13.   Loose papers are treated with a sampling method. The object is to use a small sampling of loose papers to determine the fate of a larger quantity of them. So, if a sampling of loose papers turns out to be trash, the next twelve inches of loose papers are trashed. If, on the other hand, a sampling of papers turns up documents of value, the next twelve inches of loose papers are saved. In this way, at least some portion of all the papers is reduced.

Step 14:   The crew's job is to identify important papers and turn them over to the owner. It is the owner's responsibility to process them. The owner might find the advice of a family lawyer helpful when sorting through important papers.

Identify a body double from within your crew

It's ideal if a body double emerges from the crew. This may be the supervisor or one of the assistants. A person who has had the experience of organizing your clutter and working with you is ideally suited to continue on as a body double.

Teleconsulting

For many chronically disorganized people, the fear or the experience of humiliation or embarrassment is a great obstacle to seeking organizing help. Under these circumstances, a social organizing method called teleconsulting can be very helpful. Because it is done by telephone (and sometimes supplemented with fax and e-mail communication), teleconsulting gives you the benefit of social organizing without someone actually being present in your home or office. Teleconsulting is best used for small-scale, well-defined organizing projects that do not require hands-on, physical assistance.

Because it is a structured dialogue, a teleconsult is very different from a telephone conversation. Engage in teleconsulting with a professional organizer, who can walk you through a series of questions designed to put you at ease, gather relevant information, and, depending on your responses, indicate specific steps for you to take toward your organizing goal. The teleconsultant guides you from one successful step to the next. As long as you are candid on the phone about your progress, the teleconsultant can act as your organizing partner.

I recently conducted a series of teleconsulting sessions with a chronically disorganized woman. With the woman's blessings and with my encouragement, her roommate listened in on the teleconsulting sessions on the phone extension. The roommate did not participate in the teleconsulting calls, but, because she was privy to them, the chronically disorganized person garnered two organizing partners: her teleconsultant and her roommate who was willing to be a body double.

Teleconsulting can also be helpful if you live in an area where there are no professional organizers or others who can help you. It can transform even the most disheartening, isolated organizing experience into an uplifting, social one.

Coaching

Coaching is a type of social organizing that is gaining popularity. You, as the chronically disorganized person, and the coach essentially form a team. The team formulates well-defined goals to be achieved according to an agreed upon timetable. These goals are then broken down into smaller objectives. You agree to be held accountable to achieving these objectives according to the timetable. The coach monitors progress, troubleshoots, and provides encouragement and support all along the way via regular, structured communication. Coaching can be done in person, by phone, or with a combination of both. The most important element of a coaching relationship is accountability – doing what you say you will do, when you say you will do it.

It can be a relief to be held accountable to someone. I regularly coach a chronically disorganized woman who is a writer. Writing is a particularly solitary activity. "Because I have nobody looking over my shoulder, telling me I must write, I wait until the last minute. But the stress of writing this way is affecting my health. My blood pressure is high and I have an ulcer."

Joan and I have broken her writing deadlines down into actual pages per week she must write. She "punches in" with me each day via e-mail. I send her a daily affirmation by fax as encouragement. She writes her daily page quota, then "punches out" with an e-mail to me. On a weekly phone call, we tally up the pages and adjust her writing schedule so she can be sure to meet her deadlines with as little stress as possible.

The Professional Organizer

A professional organizer is an ideal choice for performing social organizing. Professional organizers are organizing experts and can help you explore a range of solutions best suited to your particular needs. They are objective and will not judge you or your character. You can easily locate a professional organizer in your area by contacting the National Association of Professional Organizers (NAPO) or The National Study Group on Chronic Disorganization (NSGCD). Both groups are listed in the Resource section of this book.

There is a very powerful television commercial about an alcohol treatment center. The commercial does its best to advertise and promote the center, but at the end of the commercial a voice says, "If you do not get help at our center, please, get help somewhere." Whether you choose to use a professional organizer, body double, crew, tele-consultant, or coach, always organize socially.

THE DAILY CHRONICAL

Esther's newspaper collection fills her basement. Each Sunday she rolls up a week's worth of unread newspapers and stuffs them into a paper bag. The paper bags stand in long rows on the base-ment floor, lined up like disciplined little soldiers. A single file of them troops up the basement stairs, meets in formation in the laundry room, and stands there at attention. Bags of newspapers fill the den and a new squadron has begun to form in the guest bath-room. The bags of newspapers total seventy-one. Esther thinks her out-of-town guests, who will be arriving for an extended stay a month from now, might not appreciate the excessive reading mate-rial, and so she has called me.

"I'm very certain I want to live without these newspapers," Esther says emphatically. "It is not a decision I am at all conflicted about. And yet, I cannot bring myself to just throw them away."

Organizing In-Absentia

An effective social organizing method for Esther to use is called Organizing In-Absentia. This is a fancy name for organizing which proceeds without the presence of the chronically disorganized person at all. Chronically disorganized people like Esther often have a very clear vision of the organizing objectives they hope to achieve. At the same time they are often aware that their chronic disorganization is the major obstacle standing in the way of reaching that objective.

If Esther's organizing objective is to be achieved, the only way to resolve this dilemma is for her to exempt herself from the organizing process. Organizing In-Absentia is the only option available.

Esther is a consummate fund-raiser and a community activist. The modest research value of the newspapers, coupled with Esther's natural thirst for knowledge, has induced her to save all the newspapers, even though somewhere in the deep recesses of her mind she knows she will never find the time to go back and read them all, let alone clip and file the most important columns.

Newspapers are like a tar pit for chronically disorganized people. Their subject matter is diverse and wide ranging, appealing to the "infomania" in so many chronically disorganized people. **Infomania is the joy of indulging in simultaneous, diverse interests from any and all sources**. Newspapers come like the sun, are inexpensive, and are by far the easiest reading material to acquire. You can neglect them for months and still they will come, eternally forgiving and forever loyal.

The information in newspapers is obsolete about eight hours after it is published. Over 70% of a newspaper is advertising. Of the 30% of real news and information, 80% can be accessed with ease through other kinds of media, like radio or TV. 100% is obtainable over the Internet. A good 50% of any newspaper will repeat in some form the very next day. A newspaper unread, is closer to trash than orange peels.

"What if I pull out the sections I am most interested in, and read and clip just those?" Esther implores.

"Well, that would help," I respond, "but on average, the time it will take for you to sift through these bags and remove only the sections you hope to read will be about twenty minutes per bag.

Multiply that times the seventy one bags of newspapers you own, and we're looking at almost twenty-four hours of sifting. Then there is the actual reading and clipping of the chosen sections, easily adding another two hours per bag. 165 hours ought to do it."

"It's hopeless," Esther despairs. "I certainly have better things to do with my life than sift through old newspapers, but I just can't dump them without looking through them first."

Esther's accumulations are a true compulsion. Compulsions are irresistible desires to repeat behaviors over and over again. They are psychologically rooted deeper than even our most hardened habits. I am aware that breaking a compulsive behavior like hoarding newspapers might require the assistance of a mental health professional. But there seems no harm in pushing the envelope with Esther before I suggest she may need help I cannot provide.

"I believe you when you say you cannot get rid of these newspapers. But you can make a choice here. It won't be easy, but it goes like this: either the newspapers stay, or else you go."

"Pardon?" Esther exclaims, shocked. (Remember, I warned you about the word "pardon". Esther wants to give me one more chance to prove I am not crazy.)

"What I mean is that it's your choice if the newspapers are to remain. But if you choose for the newspapers *not* to remain, it is *you* who will have to go – at least for a few hours. If you go out, say to the movies, I can dispose of the papers. Otherwise there is nothing I can do to help."

Esther needs time to think. This is not an easy choice for her. While she decides, I recommend she imagine her guests' faces when they see her welcoming home, filled with charm and comfort instead of bags of newspapers.

Three days later, Esther calls me. "Must it be a movie?" she asks finally, and I laugh out loud. Esther plans to go out to lunch with a friend and then to the store. It is important that she not return until the deed is done. When Esther returns, the bags of newspapers are gone. I am gone. Only an invoice and a rose remain.

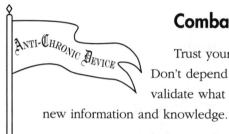

Combating Infomania

Trust your intellect and your memory. Don't depend on written information to validate what you already know. Seek only new information and knowledge.

Have someone else flag, clip, and file your magazine and newspaper articles.

Cancel magazine subscriptions that are too much alike (e.g., do you really need *Time* **and** *Newsweek*?).

Learn to skim.

Subscribe only to weekend editions of newspapers.

Immediately discard newspaper sections you never read.

Rediscover the library. Read their magazines and newspapers.

Join a clipping service.

Utilize a variety of informational sources: television, radio, cable, Internet.

Make use of on-line database and search services.

Recognize that information now becomes obsolete quicker than ever before.

Make room in your life for information yet to come rather than information that has passed you by.

SOCIAL ORGANIZING METHODS

The Body Double

The Crew

Teleconsultants

Coaches

The Professional Organizer

Organizing In-Absentia

Family

Friends

Out Of Order: Maintaining Organizing Success

Organizing is not a one-time event; it requires ongoing maintenance. A filing system will be orderly only if files are returned to it promptly. A room will stay organized only if clothes are re-hung immediately. But if you are chronically disorganized, doing maintenance organizing by yourself can doom you before you even start. Maintenance organizing should always be done socially. There are two reasons for this. One is that chronically disorganized people tend to over-organize maintenance chores. And the second reason is that it is during maintenance organizing that most chronically disorganized people tend to go off-task. Doing maintenance organizing with someone else mitigates against over-organizing and going off-task.

OVER-ORGANIZING

"I can spend hours refiling folders back into the filing cabinet," notes Fran. "I like to look inside each folder, and make sure all the papers are facing the same way. I might even write up new labels for each folder. These perfectionist tasks swallow up so much time, I never finish the simple chore of putting my files back into the cabinet."

Over-organizing of the kind Fran describes is very easy to fall prey to during maintenance. Maintenance tasks are deceptively simple. There is nothing complicated about refiling folders or hanging up clothes. In fact, maintenance organizing can be downright boring. Chronically disorganized people often attempt to inject interest, excellence, or satisfaction into maintenance organizing to compensate for this dullness.

But this spirit is misplaced. Maintenance is supposed to be a little dull. It is not something meant to be challenging. Instead of doing only what is required, over-organizing soon turns simple maintenance into a time-consuming project. The result is that over-organizing sabotages maintenance organizing. Once that happens, whatever organizing gains are made are wiped out and disorganization recurs.

But the practice of doing maintenance organizing with someone rather than alone prevents over-organizing. The presence of this second person, either as an active helper or a body double, commits not one, but two people to what is essentially a simple job. Thus, in some sense the task is already over-organized. This social element added to maintenance organizing speeds it up, counteracting boredom, and assuring that the inherent simplicity of maintenance organizing is preserved.

"I used to separate all my unopened mail into neat stacks of bills, solicitations, personal letters, bank and investment statements, subscriptions, and so forth. Then I would carefully open every single envelope, even if I knew it was junk mail. After that, I'd pull out the contents of all of the envelopes and read each insert (did you know, the average credit card bill contains three inserts?). Now I process my mail every day with my secretary. We trash the junk mail unopened, and quickly pull out the bills to be paid and statements to be reviewed. When I do my mail daily with my secretary, it never piles up and it's just not a big deal anymore," observes Richard.

GOING OFF-TASK

The conditions for going off-task are ripe during maintenance organizing. Usually you are by yourself. The maintenance organizing before you seems easy enough to perform, so easy, in fact, your mind is free to wander. And you let it. You let your mind take you from this task to that task and, pretty soon, everything but the task at hand is being accomplished. That is called going off-task.

"I set out to hang up my clothes in the bedroom closet and end up doing organizing or cleaning in every room of the house," notes Grace. "For instance, I'll find a dish towel in the bedroom closet that belongs in the kitchen and so I'll take it to the kitchen, and while I'm in the kitchen I'll put the dirty dishes in the dishwasher. Because my hands are now a little dirty, I'll go into the bathroom to wash my hands and end up cleaning the bathroom mirror. Eventually I'll remember I originally intended to hang up the clothes in the bedroom, but now I've run out of time."

Going off-task gobbles up time, leaving maintenance organizing incomplete. That is why it is best to set up regular maintenance appointments with yourself. The key word here is "regular". The regularity of maintenance appointments confers integrity and priority to the organizing task at hand. For instance, when you take your car in regularly for an oil change, you do not expect a new paint job or your brakes to be fixed. You only expect your oil to be changed because that is what the appointment is dedicated to.

The same is true of maintenance organizing. Regular maintenance appointments provide the external discipline, priority, and focus needed to insure that the temptation to go off-task is prevented. They are the most important anti-chronic device you have for preserving organizing success, especially when conducted with another person.

THE BODY DOUBLE

Body doubling is a great maintenance technique. Let's say you have just finished organizing a very disorganized closet. Of course you realize that a little regular upkeep will keep the closet organized. At least once a season, arrange for a body double to come to your home. You can gather up clothes and other items from around the house that belong in the closet. Now is also the time for you to pack off-season clothes away, hang up current season clothes, and remove unwanted items from the closet. Notice that you are doing the maintenance organizing. And what is your body double doing? Body doubling. Your body double is working on an organizing chore close by, in your range of sight, but not directly organizing the closet with you. Without distracting you, your body double is perhaps folding clothes or packing items into cartons, or maybe doing something completely unrelated to your closets!

Bill paying is a another good example. Chronically disorganized people understand that bill paying is a crucial organizing task all adults must undertake. Yet they procrastinate and procrastinate because bill paying is especially dull, or maybe they have some other reason (or excuse!). Pretty soon the pile of bills is huge, late fees and finance charges accrue, and tracking expenditures or picking up billing errors is nearly impossible. A body double does not pay the bills. You do. But sitting close by, a regularly scheduled body double will create the context in which you can do such organizing chores.

OTHER MAINTENANCE SUPPORT

A mother and her ten-year-old child show up at Iris' office every ten days. The pair sit at Iris' conference room table and untangle her overhead transparencies, handouts, and trade show materials. "This chore used to take me hours. I'd return from attending a three day trade show or conducting five workshops in a row, and I'd go crazy trying to get all this stuff back together again. Now my two assistants do the job for me," Iris says with pride.

Janet, on her long drive home from distant sales calls, dictates the information about her newly gathered business contacts into a microcassette. She has hired a young blind man to transcribe the recordings directly into her database on the 30th of every month. A woman with hearing impairments does all Janet's mailings, restocks the sales literature in her car, and deletes returned mail from her database.

Alice owns over 1,000 greeting cards. A world traveler, she buys greeting cards in many languages from all over the world and sends them to her worldwide friends, business colleagues, and family. On my recommendation, Alice brought the huge collection to a local senior citizens' club. They turned the jumbled mass of greeting cards into well organized trays, divided by occasions, and returned them to Alice.

Now Alice selects the cards she wants to send to various people, fills in her personal messages, and addresses the envelopes. Once a week, a club member comes to her door to pick up the addressed cards. She attaches return address labels and takes the cards to the post office. Once a month, a club member arrives at Alice's house to organize the newest greeting cards into Alice's trays. In return for this maintenance support, Alice reimburses the seniors for expenses and sends their club a generous annual contribution.

Pete and his administrative assistant, Lois, do maintenance organizing together. "I could not administratively support Pete in the past because he was too disorganized to make use of me," observes Lois. "Now that I've learned how he organizes, each Friday, like clockwork, we make up Pete's to-do list for the upcoming week; we refile folders that have been pulled from the filing cabinet; and we pull the files we will need for the next week. It's not the most interesting work in the world, but the office and Pete stay organized."

Maintenance support is all around you. A list of sources appears below.

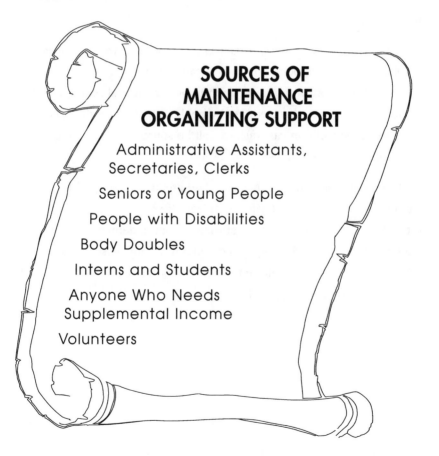

SOURCES OF MAINTENANCE ORGANIZING SUPPORT

Administrative Assistants, Secretaries, Clerks

Seniors or Young People

People with Disabilities

Body Doubles

Interns and Students

Anyone Who Needs Supplemental Income

Volunteers

Conclusion

If your personal history has been dominated by chronic disorganization, conquering it will not happen overnight, but it can be done. To do so requires that you, first and foremost, ignore the myth of "once and for all." Conventional organizing methods are not effective for all, and organizing is never done just once. Unconventional organizing methods, especially those that embrace emotions, respect the influence of learning styles on organizing style, and tend to be wholistic, are your most potent weapons for conquering chronic disorganization.

If you look for a model of organizing only among well-organized people, you will disappoint yourself. Because you organize unconventionally, seek organizing inspiration in non-traditional settings. An efficient supermarket, the user-friendly book store, the colorful classroom, even the well-run car wash can all be sources of organizing ideas and practical solutions.

Don't confront your enemy alone. Use an army of support for getting organized and for staying organized. If you use the methods in this book, you will keep disorganization from undermining your quality of life. But **staying** organized will never come easy and so you must use the most significant self-help tool that exists – your ability to ask for and accept help.

ABOUT THE AUTHOR

A native New Yorker, Judith Kolberg is a graduate of the State University of New York at Binghamton, with a degree in sociology. She came to the South as a professional political organizer, supplementing her income as an office manager and executive secretary. Drawing on her experience in politics and office management, Ms. Kolberg founded FileHeads Professional Organizers in 1989 in Atlanta, Georgia.

Ms. Kolberg is the recipient of the National Association of Professional Organizer's Founders' Award. In addition to writing, she is a consultant, trainer, and public speaker and directs the National Study Group on Chronic Disorganization. Ms. Kolberg is currently writing a book on radical time management. She remains active in politics.

Resources about Chronic Disorganization

Conquering Chronic Disorganization
Judith Kolberg
Groundbreaking, organizing methods proven to end chronic disorganization, presented in a fun-to-read, easy-to-implement format.
"I highly recommend this book to disorganized people, their loved ones, and the people who try to help them." – Jerri Udelson, VP International Coach Federation, NE
$13.00, Paperback, ISBN 0-9667970-0-0, 135pp, 5 1/2 x 8 1/2

Surviving Chronic Disorganization
Judith Kolberg
A humorous and educational audio cassette tape filled with practical advice and inspiration for anyone who struggles with getting organized. "If you think getting organized is just about file cabinets and neat cupboards, listen to this tape! Its perfect for folks who don't fit the mold..." -- Barbara Hemphill, *Taming The Paper Tiger*
$13.00, Audio cassette tape (30 min.) and companion guide 12pp, spiral bound

What Every Professional Organizer Needs to Know About Chronic Disorganization
Judith Kolberg
An indispensable resource for anyone who wants to explore new and innovative organizing techniques proven to be effective with chronically disorganized people.
"...engaging and exciting approaches that go to the heart of how people who are frustrated and demoralized by organizing challenges can be understood and helped." -- Sari Solden, *Women With Attention Deficit Disorder*
$13.00, 70pps, spiral bound, 6x9

ORDER FORM

Please send me *Conquering Chronic Disorganization*

_____copies @ $13.00 each $_____

Surviving Chronic Disorganization

_____copies @ $13.00 each $_____

*What Every Professional Organizer Needs
to Know About Chronic Disorganization*

_____copies @ $13.00 each $_____

SPECIAL OFFER!! ALL THREE PRODUCTS

FOR JUST $35.00!!! $_____

Add $3.00 shipping and handling for any one or two products
and $4.00 shipping and handling for any three products
$_____

TOTAL ENCLOSED $_____

Make checks payable to Judith Kolberg

Mail to :

Squall Press, Inc.   Phone: 404-289-1622

P. O. Box 691

Decatur, GA 30031   Email: Worthchat@aol.com

Helpful Organizations

FileHeads Professional Organizers provides on-site consulting, and teleconsulting to disorganized individuals and specializes with those who are chronically disorganized; conducts workshops on organizational skills for employers, mental health professionals, ADD coaches, and professional organizers, and sells books, tapes and other products about chronic disorganization.
1142 Chatsworth Drive, Avondale Estates, GA 30002,
404-231-6172, Worthchat@aol.com

The National Association of Professional Organizers (NAPO) is the professional membership organization of professional organizers. NAPO provides referrals to individuals seeking a professional organizer; educates the public about the field of professional organizing; and provides education and training to professional organizers.
1033 La Posado Drive, Suite 220, Austin, TX 78752-3824,
512-454-8626 napo@assnmgmt.com, www.napo.net

The National Study Group on Chronic Disorganization (NSGCD) is a membership organization of professional organizers who share a special interest in chronic disorganization. The NSGCD makes referrals to individuals seeking a professional organizer with a specialty in chronic disorganization; provides education and information about chronic disorganization to professionals in many fields; and publishes the *Reading and Resource List* and other products for individuals who are chronically disorganized.
NSGCD c/o Judith Kolberg, Director
1142 Chatsworth Drive, Avondale Estates, GA 30002, 404-231-6172

American Coaching Association helps individuals with Attention Deficit Disorder (ADD) locate a coach in their area; trains people who want to become coaches; and is a professional membership organization of ADD coaches. P.O. Box 353 Lafayette Hill, PA 19444
610-825-4505, e-mail: 75471.3101@compuserve.com,
www.americoach.com

Messies Anonymous is a nationwide network of support groups; publishes a newsletter; sells books and other products helpful to disorganized people; and operates a Clutter Buddy program. Send a self-addressed stamped envelope for more information to
5025 SW 114 Ave., Miami, FL 33165, www.messies.com

OC Foundation provides information about obsessive compulsive disorder and assists people in contacting a mental health professional in their area. OC Foundation, PO Box 70, Milford, CT 06460,
(203) 878-5669

Helpful Products

3M, 3M Center Bldg., 223-3S-03, St. Paul, MN 55144, 1-800-364-3577, www.3M.com. Post-It Notes

20th Century Plastics, PO Box 2393, Brea, CA 92822, 800-767-0777, fax: 800-786-7939. Sheet protectors, clear and transparent file folders, poly bags

Esselte Corporation, Clinton Road, Garden City, NY 11530, 800-645-6051, http://www.esselte.com. Crates on casters, colored file folders, vertical file folder holders

Get Organized, 600 Cedar Hollow Road, Paoli, PA 19301, 800-803-9400, www.getorginc.com. Catalogue of organizing products for the home, http://www.getorginc.com

Lego Systems™, 800-422-5346, www.lego.com. Plastic toy blocks

Monaco HangUp Bags, Box 40, Bethel, CT 06801, 800-448-4877, fax: 203-744-3228, monaco@hangupbags.com. Plastic hanging bags

SBS Industries, Inc., 83 Wyldewood Rd, Easton, CT 06612, 203-261-5505, fax: 203-261-9376. Plastic, see-through products for the office

Index

A

Accountability 107
Action 20,52,53,65,69,93
ADD Success Stories 89
Administrative Assistant 7,79,119
Alphabetize 7,20
Anchor 93,95
Anti-chronic device 11,21,27,32,35,36,40,55,79,81,92,
  105,111,116
Artists 68,86,87,88
Aslett, Don 82
Assistant 96,97,100,101
Attention Deficit Disorder 56,89,122,123
Auditory 43-47,64,65,71
Awards 23,82

B

Beauty 32,34,35,102
Bibliobolic 28
Big Bag Floor Rack 70
Binders 3,64
Body Double 93-96,105,106,108,112,115,117,119
Books 28-30,83,84,97-101,123
Boredom 115
Breaking things down 73,79
Brown, Denslow 81
Business Cards 53,86,87

C

Calls 15,19,54,61,77,106
Catalogues 37,83,85,93,124
Categorize 48
Centers 21,53,54,64
Charity 26,44,100,104
Checklists 81
Chronic Disorganization 6-12,37,43,53,92-98,105-108,
  114,120-125
Clear 67-71,122
Clipboards 62,64

K

Keepsakes 82
Kinesthetic 43,48,51-53,55,58,59,62,64,65,71
Kinetic Sympathy 37-40

L

Learning style 43,46,59,65,71,120
Legos™ 62,63,125
Literacy Volunteers 30
Logic 9,10,21,32,33,37,55,89

M

Magazines 33,36,37,80,83,84,85,90,93,98,102,103,111
Mail 37,53,58,66,93,94,95,115,118
Maintain 21,37,41,79,92,93
Mementos 28,82
Memorabilia 36,98
Memory 45,65,111
Mental 12,48,56,74,85,110,124
Methods 8,10,11,29,31,34,37,71,73,74,85,87,92,99,102,104,
    105,108,120,122
Microcassette recorder 46,47,118
Models 62,81,95,96,120
Morale 92
Moving 101
Muttering 14-21
Myth 10,120

N

National Association of Professional Organizers 107,121,124
National Study Group on Chronic Disorganization 107,121,124
Need
    low 28
    high 28,29,31
Negotiations 27,40
Neurological 10,43,48,67
Newspapers 33,83,108-111
Noise 46,58,64
    external 56,57
    internal 56,57

O

Obsessive compulsive disorder 12,23,124
Off-task 114-116
Organizing
    auditory 43-47,64,65,71
    big picture 67,73
    conventional 9-11,38,43,55,73,120
    emotional 10,16,19-28,32,33,37,39,67,92,120
    in-absentia 108-109
    kinesthetic 43,48,51-53,55,58,59,62,64,65,71
    maintenance 114-119
    over 114-115
    radical 11,37
    social 92,93,97,101,105-108,112,114
    skills 10,88,96,124
    styles 65,71,92,120
    unconventional 9,10,11,16,19,22,23,32,53,68,71,120
    visual 16,43,47,48,65-75,89
    whole 73,74,79
    wholistic 73,74,81,92,120
Over-organizing 114-115

P

Packrats 23,37
Panel System 60,61,62,63
Panic Order 19,20
Papers
    financial 99,102,104
    important 99,102,105
Past, The 83-85
Pegboard 51,81
Perfectionist 114
Personalize 25
Personification 29
Photographs 83,84,85,89,98,102,104
Planner 7,57,59,60
Planning 55,85
Possessions 29,34,37,55,82,97
Post-It Notes™ 65,125

Present, The 83,85
Presort 97-104
Priority 45,55,59,61,67,70,116
Productivity 51,56,58
Professional organizer 23,35,36,81,95,100,101,105,106,107,
    108,112,121,122,124
Purchasing 41,82

Q
Quality of life 6,7,8,9,13,93,120
Quantum Learning 52

R
Raabe, Tom 28
Radical organizing 11,37
Recommended Refuse 98-102
Recycle 5,26,84,99,103
Residential clutter 6
Retrieve 10,19,22,34
Reveal 68,69,70,71
Rolodex™ 53,86
Rummage 48,50,51

S
Sampling 98,99,102,104
Saving 4,5,23,24,34,82
Schedule 57,70,73,84,85,107,117
Secretary 45,81,115
Self-Help 120
Seniors 118,119
Signal 32
Social organizing 92,93,97,101,105-108,112,114
Space Travel 80,90
Stationery supplies 98,102
Student 100,101,119
Styles, Learning 43,46,59,65,71,92,120
Styles, Organizing 65,71,92
Subcategorize 48

T

Tactile 61
Tangential 22,56
Tax documents 20,83,84,99,102,104
Teleconsult 105,108,112,124
Themes 74,76,79-83,85,90
Time 7,55,58,59,60,61,63,70,85,106
Timeline 70,85,90
Time Management 9,55,56,58,59,60,61,70,71,73,80,85
To-do 56,58,59,60,62,63,73,119
Topics 9
Transparency 65,67,70
Transparent 67,71,125
Treasure 18,33,34,35

U

Unconventional organizing 9,10,11,16,19,22,23,32,53,68,71,120
Useful 32,33
Utility 32,33,34

V

Verb 51-55
Vertical 19,20,59,125
Visual 16,43,47,48,65-75,89
Visual field 75

W

Wholistic 73,74,81,92,120
Writers 86,90,107